Keeping
Entertaining
Simple

Keeping Entertaining Simple

500 Tips for
Carefree Gatherings
with Family & Friends

Martha Storey

STOREY
BOOKS
Schoolhouse Road
Pownal, Vermont 05261

*The mission of Storey Communications is to serve
our customers by publishing practical information
that encourages personal independence
in harmony with the environment.*

Edited by Aimee Poirier
Cover design by Meredith Maker
Cover illustration by Laura Tedeschi
Text design by Susan Bernier
Production assistance by Eileen Clawson
Line drawings by Martha Storey
Indexed by Nan Badgett, Word•a•bil•i•ty

Recipe on page 110 adapted from *Making Gingerbread Houses,* A
Storey Country Wisdom Bulletin.

    The information in this book is true and complete to the best of
our knowledge. All recommendations are made without guarantee on
the part of the author or Storey Communications, Inc. The author
and publisher disclaim any liability in connection with the use of this
information. For additional information, please contact Storey
Communications, Inc., Schoolhouse Road, Pownal, Vermont 05261.
    Storey Books are available for special premium and promotional
uses and for customized editions. For further information, please call
the Custom Publishing Department at 1-800-793-9396.

Printed in the United States by Vicks Lithograph
10 9 8 7 6 5 4 3 2 1

Library of Congress Cataloging-in-Publication Data

Storey, Martha, 1944-
    Keeping entertaining simple / by Martha Storey.
        p.   cm.
    Includes index.
    ISBN 1-58017-056-0 (pb : alk. paper)
    1. Entertaining. 2. Cookery. I. Title.
TX731.S74   1998
642'.4—dc21   97-3435
                                                                CIP

Contents

Dedication

This book is dedicated to my husband, John.
He has truly been my partner, my best friend,
and my inspiration for most of my life.

~

Thanks

A big "thank you" to all of my friends at Storey who
shared their ideas with me. I promised each of them a
jar of *Martha's Homemade Fudge Sauce* if they helped,
and it looks like I will be busy cooking for a while!

Introduction

W hile thinking in depth about the subject of "entertaining simply," I realized that these two words may indeed be at odds. To *entertain* means to engage, occupy, engross, absorb, enliven, even gratify. If you entertain, you host, welcome, regale, have company, fête, and celebrate! *Simply* means easily, plainly, even artlessly. So to *entertain with simplicity* can mean hosting modestly, sparely, with no adornments or embellishments. Sound like fun? Not to me!

When I entertain, I do want to have fun, and of course to make sure that my guests have a terrific time as well. I want to serve great food, have fresh flowers everywhere, good music, and a comfortable setting so that my friends can relax and enjoy a special evening out.

The catch here is that I don't want to spend weeks, days, or even too many hours preparing for my company. Not that I don't enjoy cooking and the fun of preparations. In fact, I do a lot of things from scratch. I grow and can my own vegetables, make jams and jellies from my own berry bushes, make homemade pasta, bake bread and apple-cinnamon pies to take advantage of my apple trees! But I entertain often, and, quite frankly, I am usually too busy to interrupt my normal routine for all of these special touches. Since I do want to entertain, see my friends and family, and even enjoy myself, I try to do it simply, with little stress and little disruption. I find being spontaneous is an easy way for me to approach an event. Less time to prepare equals less stress on me, and a lot more fun.

Of course, not everyone feels this way, and I certainly admire those who can regularly host a dinner party for 12, send out wonderful invitations a month in advance, serve six courses without breaking a sweat, and have the house and bathrooms smelling like a tropical rain forest when their guests arrive. My hat is off to them!

But I usually need help, of one sort or another, and if you have bought this book for yourself you probably do, too. You most likely:

- ◆ Work, in or out of your home
- ◆ Have a family who wants your extra attention when you are not working
- ◆ Have limited time, energy, and perhaps financial resources
- ◆ Enjoy seeing other people once in a while

If so, let me assure you that entertaining *can* be simple, and simply wonderful for everyone involved. All you need to do is think creatively, plan a little, know your own limits, and delegate.

Before you plan your next party, ask yourself, "How can I do it so that I have fun?" There are many other questions that you need to answer as well:

- What about the piles of stuff in the living room?
- What can I do with the kids?
- What can I serve that is delicious, quick, and easy?
- Is there a way to get some help?
- How can I cut costs, yet make the evening attractive?
- How can I enjoy it myself?

While I may not be Martha Stewart with a staff of hundreds, I do have lots of friends who were willing to share some of their tips on this subject. I also have two talented daughters, Jennifer Gillis and Jessica Dils, busy young mothers who can both help me pull a party together more quickly than any professional caterers I know. In fact, they have been quite instrumental in the writing of this book (that's where my own delegating comes in), sharing their time and talents with me, and now with you.

In the pages that follow, you will find a compilation of tips, tricks, and suggestions that can take some of the pressure off when you entertain.

Some may be obvious, but many are wonderfully creative. This book shouldn't take long to read. In fact, my hope is that you'll pick it up just about anytime or anywhere and get a quick tip that can help you plan your next party with more ease and less stress. We hope you enjoy it, and happy entertaining!

Nature is pleased with simplicity.

Isaac Newton

Simple Ways of Celebrating

The simple truth is that it doesn't take a million dollars or a million ideas to be a great host. While some of us may be overwhelmed by the idea of entertaining or come up with many reasons why we can't do so, when it comes right down to it, there are far more good reasons for getting our friends and family together on a regular basis.

I remember once hosting a chili party for old and new neighbors in our area, complete with 12 children (all of whom were under 5). As my husband and I scurried around before the big hour, trying to keep our own children out from under foot and happy (we didn't want to greet our friends with tear-stained kids), I wondered if it was all worth it.

But as the evening got underway and we had a chance to finally see our friends and have meaningful conversations with everyone, I changed my mind. And as the other parents and neighbors left, thanking us over and over for "hosting" the evening, I knew that entertaining was definitely worth it. And it was relatively simple. Now, I know it's not as simple as hitting the drive-through at McDonald's, but it certainly is rewarding and fun.

The key to keeping your entertaining simple is to have a simple plan. You may not always stick to it, but at least you won't get overwhelmed before you even begin. It is easy, especially when it comes to hosting an event or party, to put it off for one reason or another: My kids are too little. My kids are too big. My house is too little. My cooking is too basic. My dogs are out of control. My family room smells like kitty litter. Who would want to come? I can never come up with a great idea that's never been done.

Well, this chapter is full of ideas for you to call your own. You can borrow from the theme party ideas or let them spark an idea of your own. Great entertainers love to be borrowed from, as long as it is not the same party your neighbor threw last weekend! Imitation is the ultimate compliment, so feel free to admire and "borrow" other people's ideas freely.

Most of my favorite tried-and-true recipes have come from other people's parties, and I can honestly say my friends are flattered when they taste the same dish at my house. "Is this my apple pie recipe? It always seems to taste better when someone else makes it!" It will certainly simplify your life, and why should a great idea have to be discovered twice?

And remember, no matter where you get your ideas for entertaining, you will make them your own just by being you. Your own style and flair will shine through no matter how or where or when you entertain, so grab an idea and start entertaining. It's simple!

Save Money, Yet Still Have Your Kind of Party

Save money by keeping away from meat, fish, and alcohol. Pasta, soups, homemade breads and desserts, beer, wine, lemonade, and iced tea are all great, and much less expensive, alternatives. It's not fun for you if you break the bank every time you entertain.

Make parties BYOB whenever possible. People understand how expensive liquor can be for a whole party. When someone asks what they can bring, say, "How about a bottle of wine?" Then make sure to point it out to others. Inform your guests that "Sally and Bob brought this wonderful wine."

Add your own decorative touches with little effort and money. Add a dusting of powdered sugar and some fresh fruit like grapes or cherries, instead of icing, to a cake. It's healthy, too!

Make a couple of alcoholic punches instead of serving cocktails. It will save you a lot of money. Here are just a few to try.

Cranberry Fizz

- 1 quart cranberry juice
- 1 quart orange juice
- 1 quart club soda
- 1½ cups vodka (optional)

Float an ice ring in the bowl that has fresh cranberries and orange slices frozen in it to help keep it cold and to add a decorative touch. For a variation, you can use pineapple juice and orange juice, or grapefruit juice and orange juice with the appropriate fruit in the ice ring.

16 SERVINGS

Hot Mulled Cider

- 2 cinnamon sticks
- 12 whole cloves
- ½ teaspoon allspice
- 1 gallon cider
- 2 cups bourbon (optional)

Make a small gauze bag filled with the spices. Place the spice bag in the cider and heat until hot. Let simmer for 30 minutes so that the spices can permeate the cider. Add bourbon before serving if desired. Serve piping hot.

12–14 SERVINGS

Lime-Rum Punch

Chill 1 small bottle of real lime juice and a 46-ounce can of pineapple juice. Add 3 cans frozen limeade, 3 cans water, 1 fifth light rum, and 1 quart ginger ale or club soda. Mix well, adding thin slices of lime to the bowl. Serve over ice cubes in 5-ounce cups.

25 SERVINGS

Inexpensive, easy-to-make mixes such as brownies, cookies, cakes, and puddings are great for dessert. Keep them on hand.

～

Potluck is a great way to cut costs. People love to bring their specialties, and this way one person doesn't need to spend a lot of money to feed everyone. By asking each guest to bring a different course, you can easily have a full meal, complete with entrées, salads, and desserts.

～

Try having guests for meals other than dinner. Breakfast, brunch, and lunch can be easier, less expensive, and a bit more casual, but just as much fun. (See chapter 4 for ideas.)

Theme Parties

Planning a party around a theme can quickly get people inspired. If there is something to do besides eating and drinking, you can have even more fun, get to know people differently, and even save some money. We often eat more and drink more because we feel uncomfortable or even bored at some gatherings. Participating in a special activity can get us involved, keep our bodies and minds moving, and be a great icebreaker.

Before Christmas one year, a friend of mine invited a group to her house to write their Christmas cards. Everyone brought boxes of cards and an address book. We gave each other our cards, saving postage on those, and sat around drinking hot chocolate and eating carrot cake while we filled out the rest. The party turned what could have been a real chore into a relaxed, enjoyable event, and it required almost no preparation.

~

Host a pancake breakfast and then go on a Saturday-morning outing. You can spend your time together apple picking, hiking, biking, or antiquing.

~

If you and your friends share a common interest in major sporting events, host gatherings using these as the focus. "Breakfast at Wimbledon," "Super Bowl Subs," "World Series Barbecue," and "Potluck Olympics" are just a few ideas.

~

If someone in the family is involved in an event such as a soccer game, Little League, a piano recital, or ice skating, celebrate his abilities with a party that reflects his tastes in food and friends.

~

If it makes sense to invite the whole team back to your home for a celebration, do so, but keep it simple by serving just one thing, like pizza or ice cream sundaes or hot dogs from the grill.

Host "work days." All of us have big jobs that need to be accomplished, such as painting the garage, assembling a swing set, or planting the cooperative garden. So invite your close friends over for the day. After all of the work is finished, you can serve some fun food, and then plan a work day at another house next month. It's fun, inexpensive, and a good way to get a lot of big jobs done quickly. The saying "Many hands make light work" is true.

~

Wedding and baby showers need not be extravagant in order to be appreciated. Hosting one for a family member or friend brings people together for a joyous celebration, and it can be fun and simple. One bridal shower I hosted with my two daughters was a terrific success; each person brought a "kitchen-type" gift, as well as five of his or her favorite recipes to be collected into a special recipe box and given to the bride. The meal was a brunch buffet, and all of the dishes were made ahead of time, leaving plenty of time for us hosts to enjoy the gift exchange and conversations. The bride was ecstatic with her dozens of recipes!

KNOW YOUR GUESTS

By keeping the crowd in mind, you can save yourself a lot of time and money. Some folks do not need frills. They just like to celebrate.

For a baby shower, serve food that is really healthy and appropriate for a new mother to eat. Make it rich in calcium, heavy in the fruit and vegetable area, and low in fat, if possible. Ask people to bring gift certificates for the new mom, in addition to gifts for the baby. These can be for services they can perform: housecleaning for a month, baby-sitting for several hours a week, errands for a week, free dinners to put in her freezer, child care for older siblings, a personal manicure, shampoo, or five free back rubs. These can be fun, add to the festivities, and cement friendships for a lifetime.

~

Book club entertaining is simple and inspiring. Generate a group of readers who enjoy discussing what they read, and agree to gather once a month at one member's house. Keep the focus on the book and the conversation, not the cleanliness of the house or any fancy meal. Serve coffee, tea, cookies, breads, or muffins, and you've got plenty to satisfy your readers.

~

Host an international theme party. Choose a country on which you'd like to center your meal, and ask each guest to bring a particular special course. Choose appropriate music, pick colored paper napkins (red, white, and green for Italy, for instance), and have fun! A group of friends we know enjoys a regular meal-a-month arrangement, each time featuring a particular cuisine. Each person cooks something Mexican or Italian or French, and the group gathers at a different house each month, with the host setting the theme and assigning the basics.

~

Host a beer- or wine-tasting party. Each person can bring a bottle of wine or an unusual type of beer. The accompanying food can be just nice appetizers, imported cheese with fancy crackers, or unusual veggies presented on pretty platters.

~

How about a game party? This is a very low-maintenance get-together, especially if small talk is not your thing. Grab the game boards, pick some teams, put out some munchies, and go! You can even offer simple prizes to keep things lively.

~

Have a zucchini party. At the end of the summer, when zukes are much too plentiful, have everyone bring his or her favorite zucchini dish along with copies of the recipe; you provide the barbecued chicken. There are hundreds of ways to fix zucchini, from pickles to dips, breads, casseroles, and chocolate cakes and cookies. What fun! You can even hold a contest for the biggest zucchini or the best-carved zuke.

~

Be nostalgic. Ask everyone to bring something his or her grandmother used to make, or might have made. Doesn't matter if it's fattening. Once in a while it's okay to splurge!

Bring back the cocktail party. Making lots of small hors d'oeuvres in advance and freezing them helps make preparations on the day of the party much simpler. You can hold it earlier in the evening and have plenty of time to clean up and even relax afterward, since people tend to leave early. Your bar should include nonalcoholic options as well, and be sure to have plenty of nibbles.

~

Host a "boxed lunch" by inviting couples to bring a picnic for two people, including the eating utensils and napkins. The meals can be fancy or plain, hot or cold, multicourse, finger food, or fancy, but most of all they should be creative and fun. For example, use a basket and a small cloth to attractively package your meal. Then, when it is time to eat, have people bid on the boxed lunch, winning not only the meal, but the opportunity to eat with someone other than who they came with. When there are good food and good people good things happen!

~

Have an "after-the-harvest" party. Everyone brings a favorite dish of corn, or tomatoes, or whatever there is an abundance of. Or simply call your event a "harvest party" and have guests bring something that they grew or got at a farmer's market.

~

Host a "medieval meal" made up of beer and breads. Grocery stores usually offer a nice variety of breads, like sourdough, rye, pumpernickel,

FUN SPREAD IDEAS

- ◆ Cream cheese and chopped olives
- ◆ Pimiento cheese spread, jalapeño or mild
- ◆ Chopped nuts, raisins, dates, or prunes moistened with mayonnaise and lemon
- ◆ Potted ham with pickle relish, Dijon mustard, and cream cheese
- ◆ Sautéed mushrooms and onions mixed with cottage cheese
- ◆ Chicken liver sautéed with onions and garlic salt and mixed with mayonnaise
- ◆ Peanut butter, honey, and raisins

French, rosemary, onion, and more. Have unusual and tasty spreads for the bread available. You'll find some ideas in the box above. Just be creative.

~

For a fast and fun "after-the-game" party, have everyone stop at the local deli, buy a favorite sandwich, and bring it back to your house. Cut each one into four quarters and arrange them all on a large platter. Serve chips, pickles, carrot sticks, and drinks, and you've got the makings of a great new tradition. No one has spent a lot of money, there is plenty of good food, and the variety is terrific.

If you want a theme for your picnic, choose an outdoor sport, like croquet, and start a tournament that can become an annual event. Fashion a winner's plaque that can have names added each year, and keep the fun going. People look forward to each year's competition, and the winners can proudly take home the plaque until next year.

~

Host a Chinese buffet: Buy carryout for the whole group, or have each person choose and pay for a specialty, then let everyone taste and share. Develop a relationship with your favorite Chinese carryout and you may even be able to borrow some sake glasses. Use paper plates, chopsticks, and paper napkins, and the cleanup is a breeze.

~

Bring back the idea of the progressive dinner, moving from one home to the next and then the next. It's less time consuming and much less expensive than having to prepare an entire meal yourself, and it really is lots of fun. Rotate responsibilities for the different courses so that everybody gets a chance to make the entrée, hors d'oeuvres, salad, vegetables, and dessert. If your group is really excited by this, it can take all of you through an entire year of entertaining simply.

~

Host a seasonal "sugar-on-snow" party after a good snowstorm. Include fresh, warm maple syrup; when poured over fresh snow, this caramelizes and makes a gooey candy.

CHILDREN'S PARTY

Give all of your children dinner together at one house and let them have a simple party there, with several baby-sitters, while you are going from house to house.

Take advantage of local and regional specialties. Every area offers scores of unique ideas to create your own theme parties around. For example, my husband and I host an annual ice-fishing festival on Lake Champlain and wind up eating dozens of wonderful "fresh-from-the-shanty" smelts.

Try an Indian dinner with an array of exotic, spicy foods and wonderful breads. Push back the furniture and eat Indian-style, with your hands, seated on the floor. Be sure to have plenty of ice water and napkins.

Host a "come-as-you-are" party. We used to do this when we were much younger, and we always had such fun. Call up several friends and say, "Come on over now! Don't change your clothes, don't do your hair, bring something from your refrigerator, and prepare for some fun!" You never know what people will bring, but this is always a great way to spark some excitement.

If you are new to an area, host your own "open house." Your neighbors will be eager to come and meet you, but entertaining may be the last thing on your mind. Send out invitations for a Saturday open house from 10 A.M. to 10 P.M., and include the line, "Bring food appropriate for the time of day you come." We tried this once and it was a great success. All we did was clean up, clear off the dining room table, put out some drinks and sturdy paper plates, sit back, relax, and wait for our new friends to arrive. Our morning started with some neighbors coming by carrying a basket of freshly baked muffins. Others added lunch items and snacks later on, and finally an informal evening dinner party (buffet-style) emerged, mostly with friends who had come from a bit farther and brought prepared dishes. This is a great way to see a lot of people and have plenty of food.

~

Try a new version of the come-as-you-are party by hosting a "come-as-you-were" party. Instruct guests to dress in the style of the specified era. A '70s bash, for instance, would provide the perfect occasion to pull that leisure suit out of the closet. Try to remember the foods that were popular then, as well as the music. You might be surprised at what your friends can remember and then do!

~

Have a neighborhood "breakfast-hopping" party. We used to do this on summer Sunday mornings. Each family cooked a different kind of breakfast food, while the neighbors came in and out; one home offered eggs and sausage, one pancakes and bacon, a third French toast. Each participating house in your neighborhood can be designated in advance, and people can travel with their plates and forks in hand to try them all. This becomes quite a feast, and no one stays at any one house for too long. Breakfast foods are simple to make and inexpensive as well. If it sounds like too much work for one person at each house, double up and use the buddy system.

~

Remember the children's story *Stone Soup*? Hold your own Stone Soup party by inviting each guest to bring one item for the soup pot. You provide the fresh bread or biscuits, and the stock and seasonings — and don't forget to include a (clean) rock. You may be surprised at just how tasty the final product is. Children will love this. Make sure you have the book on hand to read at some point during the party.

~

Throw a "tailgate party" in your yard or driveway. Each guest can serve different items (on paper plates) from his or her car: sandwich makings at one, appetizers at another, beverages at a third, and so on. Cleanup is easy, and you don't need to worry about your house. (Be sure to have a rain date picked.)

SANDWICH IDEAS

◆ Turkey breast, melted Monterey jack, Russian dressing, and celery salt on rye

◆ Egg salad made with mayo, Dijon mustard, dill, and sunflower seeds on wheat

◆ Toasted bagel with cream cheese, Dijon mustard, sliced cucumbers, and tomatoes

◆ Roast beef, cream cheese, red onions, horseradish, and tomatoes on pumpernickel

◆ Ham, Swiss cheese, sweet or hot mustard, and thinly sliced green apples

◆ Chicken salad with green grapes on whole wheat

◆ Turkey, ham, provolone, roast beef, and coleslaw on a roll

◆ BBLT — bacon, fresh basil, lettuce, and tomatoes on white toast

◆ Turkey with cranberry sauce or chutney on wheat toast

◆ Veggie — lettuce or sprouts, tomatoes, cucumbers, shredded carrots, cheddar, and Dijon mustard in a pita pocket

Have a fall harvest soup buffet. Borrow three or four Crock-Pots and make a variety of hearty soups two days before your gathering. Pick up fresh breads at a local bakery. Make a salad using the convenience-packed lettuce varieties. Serve the soups right in the Crock-Pots, and your buffet is complete! Or better yet, ask three other friends to bring their favorite soups in their own Crock-Pots, and you only have to make one.

Host a sauce party! You supply the main ingredient, and your guests each bring a favorite sauce to add to the fun. You barbecue the chicken and have friends bring the sauce; you provide the ice cream and have them bring the toppings; or you cook a variety of pastas and let people create their own masterpieces.

Host a beer-brewers' party. Have each guest or couple bring a six-pack of their own brew and an item for your meal that would taste terrific with their particular beer. With the countless numbers of homebrewers and homebrew recipes around these days, you will be certain to have brews to satisfy every taste.

If there is any at all, there is enough to share.

Elizabeth Mullendore

Throw an omelette party. Have a couple of large skillets, plenty of eggs, and omelette fillings ready, then don an apron and take your guests' orders one at a time as they choose from your assortment. Serve the meal at a leisurely pace while people eat "buffet-style" from another table of breads and fruits. As long as you and your spouse don't mind cooking the omelettes, this is a great way to catch up and chat with each guest as he or she waits for the omelette to be served.

Some Omelette-Filling Ideas

- Chopped tomatoes and spinach
- Sautéed onions, zucchini, peppers, or mushrooms (sautéed before the party)
- Softened sun-dried tomatoes
- Fresh herbs (chives, cilantro, parsley, dill, basil)
- Cubed ham, sausage, bacon
- A variety of shredded and crumbled cheeses (goat, feta, Monterey jack, cheddar, cottage cheese, Boursin)
- Salsa, ketchup

GREAT REASONS TO CELEBRATE!

Winter

- First "sleddable" snowfall
- First fire in the fireplace
- Decorating the tree
- Taking down the tree
- First officially frozen skating pond

Spring

- First bulbs coming up
- Taking the grill out of storage
- Turning over the garden
- Mother's Day

Summer

- End of school
- Opening of the neighborhood pool
- Summer solstice
- Father's Day

Fall

- Leaf-raking party
- First frost
- Fresh apple cider party

A Simple Plan

Some people are born list makers, and others find this just one more burden. However you organize yourself, though, be sure that you have a plan to help you get your entertaining under way. Whether it's merely a shopping list or a full-blown battle plan for the event, just having something in writing will help you get started, stay focused, and keep calm. These are all good ingredients in simplifying your entertaining style!

Some people feel better when they are able to keep tight control of an event. This allows them to feel relaxed, knowing exactly what they will be serving, which utensils will be used, and where on the buffet everything will go. But if you are in the other camp, and are willing to accept your friends' help for a spontaneous evening, you may be surprised at how easy a party can be.

I once went to a caroling party at a good friend's house. It was potluck, and when I asked what I could bring to be helpful, the host said, "I know I'm serving a ham, but whatever you want to bring would be great. Just make sure it feeds a lot of people!" No guidance, no "dessert would be great" or "make yours an appetizer." My friend just extended the invitation and was willing to let the chips fall where they may. I loved it! Talk about simple. And when we arrived at the buffet table, there was a beautiful assortment of dishes, no two alike, not too many salads and no desserts. It was simply perfect and it started with her simple plan of "no plan at all." She enjoyed herself as much as, or more than, anyone else at the party. Take what you will from this story, but if the plan is the key to success — make it an easy one!

Planning

The keys to a stress-free evening are simple — plan ahead and do ahead. While these may sound obvious, you may not actually do them unless you remind yourself.

~

If you make a list organized by task, things won't get too overwhelming. If your errands are all over town, for instance, jot them down logically so you don't spend time driving back and forth.

~

On your list, spread out the things you need to do over several days. Make headings by the day, and check off the items as you complete them. Give yourself a break and avoid stress by not trying to do everything the day before.

Clean and organize your refrigerator regularly. If you know what is in there you won't be surprised to find an empty bottle of ketchup or soured half-and-half just when you are getting ready to serve your guests. Also, you won't have to buy more pickles if you know there are already two opened jars in the fridge.

~

Make sure you know what is in your freezer and when its freshness might expire. Food that is freezer worn is usually safe to eat, but can be quite tasteless.

WHEN PLANNING AHEAD IS IMPOSSIBLE

One of my friends found herself hosting an impromptu evening for six friends on a day when she'd gotten home from work unusually late and had no time to shop or cook. When the guests arrived, she announced that they would be having a paella party, but that "We are all going to the grocery store first . . . together!" She handed out shopping lists, the guests found and paid for their ingredients, and then they all returned to her house and started cooking. Everyone was given a task to perform, they shared a bottle of wine as they cooked, and even though dinner wasn't served until nearly 11 P.M., everyone had a wonderful time, especially the host!

If there is a great pork chop special, buy in quantity, but make a note that they should be used before the date when they will have lost all of their flavor. If you are approaching that point, plan a gathering accordingly. Throwing out food is a tremendous waste: a waste of time shopping for it in the first place, a waste of hard-earned money, and, of course, a waste of good food.

Have a plan, but don't be so rigid that you can't be spontaneous. I have found that spontaneity leads to surprises, creativity, and very positive outcomes. For example, surprise friends at their own house, with all of the guests bringing the party there. I did this for a friend who was turning 40. All the guests brought a gag gift and a low-fat dish. When we arrived at her doorstep all together, it knocked her socks off! She was touched that we cared enough to remember in such a fun way, and no one had to clean the house.

Great food and entertaining ideas can come from anywhere, anytime. Keep your eyes and ears open. Jot down the idea you heard on the radio on your way to work.

Use those magazines you subscribe to as sources of information. Don't just recycle them: Tear them apart. Keep a file, envelope, or drawer for clipped recipes that sound easy, menus that sound intriguing, even party ideas you'd like to try.

Keep lists of what you've done and served before. You can use a notebook or keep a computer file of menus that you have used successfully. If you don't have to come up with new ideas each time you entertain, you have saved yourself a good bit of time. This also allows you to remember what you served to whom, so that you don't duplicate the menu too often with the same folks.

Shopping

Many people enjoy grocery shopping, but I must admit I would rather be doing almost anything else. When I do go, I often shop just for that day or meal so that I don't have to spend much time, and so that I can buy what's the freshest. However, there are times when, like everyone else, I need to stock up on staples and do that big shopping job so that life runs relatively smoothly on a daily basis. The best advice I can give you here is to invest in a chest or upright freezer. While it might be expensive in the beginning, preparing items and freezing them for future occasions is a real time and money saver. Also, a freezer allows me to take advantage of good specials and specialty foods; it takes quite a bit of unnecessary worry out of the party equation if I know that I have something I can take out of the freezer.

THE MANY BENEFITS AND USES OF FREEZER CHESTS

"When my husband and I were in graduate school, we lived in a wonderful old apartment that had a refrigerator with limited freezer space. And while it was only the two of us, we could barely store one box of Eggos and a handful of ice cubes. So when chest freezers went on sale at the end of one summer, we decided to take the plunge. We got some friends to help us haul it up to the fourth floor, where we treated them to Popsicles. The freezer certainly didn't fit in our kitchen, but it found a nice home in our dining room/office and it was quickly put to good use. Not only did it hold plenty of easy frozen meals (perfect for impromptu entertaining), but it also served as a changing table for our son six months later!

While not all freezers become such an important, well-loved part of the family, they all certainly help keep shopping, preparing, and storing food for your family or guests more manageable. We have also saved substantially by stocking up on specials, and enjoying them throughout the year. If you have one, use it; if you don't, think about investing in one. They come in many sizes, and even if you have to keep yours in the hall closet it will be a lifesaver."

Jennifer Gillis

Write out your menu, including beverages, and use this list to compile your shopping list. Segment your list into the following categories: produce, dairy, canned goods, frozen foods, dry goods, breads, and beverages. While this may sound tedious, it will make your trip to the supermarket go much more smoothly and quickly. You will have eliminated the need for running back and forth between aisles to pick up items you forgot.

~

When you're having weekend guests, save time later on by shopping for staples the preceding weekend. Shop for the meat and fresh produce late in the week, and pick up fresh bakery goods at the last minute.

~

While I don't want to sound like an advertisement for the telephone company, use the Yellow Pages. This simple task truly can add hours to your life: You can find out about the availability of certain items before traveling to the store.

~

Think about all of your supplier resources and how they can make your life easier. Let people do for you what they do best. For instance: Can the butcher (even the supermarket butcher) prepare your meat just like you need it? I know that my knives never seem to be quite sharp enough to bone a chicken or cut the beef for stew. So I let the market butcher do it for me. Once he even boned six Cornish game hens for me while keeping them whole! There is never an extra charge, and I can get the rest of my shopping completed while he is doing the work for me. He is the expert, and I still have all 10 of my fingers!

~

Let the baker take your order for a special loaf of bread. Again, most supermarkets have an on-site bakery, and the ovens are always hot. The market is as close as your phone, and usually has a nice variety to choose from.

~

Is there someone in town known for homemade fruit pies? If so, find her and become her best friend! We have one such friend who takes our order by phone for peach praline, strawberry-rhubarb, and apple crumb pies; she has them ready for us, piping hot, at the appointed hour. Order several at a time and freeze some.

~

If there is a specialty shop nearby, use it frequently. While this may not be the least expensive way to entertain, it is efficient, and your guests will appreciate the treats. For example, we have good friends from Connecticut who are only here in town on weekends, and when we get together they always bring wonderful Italian foods from their local deli. These are specialty items that we can't get here in the country. We make a simple pasta dinner, Bob and Louise supply the delicious hors d'oeuvres, and we are immediately transported to Italy.

We have a wonderful store in a neighboring town called Astro Beef. It mainly sells quality cuts of beef, pork, poultry, and seafood in individually wrapped, flash-frozen portions to restaurants. Several times a year, though, I go and stock up on these items for my own freezer so that I can always have something fun to put on the grill in an instant. My family loves the food, and I have served crowds of up to 100 simply by opening the bags and popping the marinated chicken breasts or steaks on the grill. There are lots of suppliers all over the country that will do the same for you.

~

Have things delivered right to your home. Most folks who live in the city know about this service, and probably use it occasionally. But if you live in the suburbs or country, you may have never even asked about delivery services. If someone can bring it to your door, think of the time you could save, and remember, your time is valuable! For example, when we travel, we sometimes call a local service that will deliver to our hotel room from any restaurant in town. We call in the order, paying with a credit card, and the delivery service picks the food up and takes a standard 15 to 18 percent tip. We have a wide variety to choose from without ever leaving our hotel room. If you live in a town that has this service, use it when you have guests. Look in the phone book under "Delivery Services." It's fast, fun, and couldn't be simpler!

Use mail-order catalogs specializing in food treats. There are many top-quality catalogers these days, and they have wonderful specialties ranging from meats to main dishes and desserts. Again, you may ultimately pay more for the food, but consider the amount of time you won't have to spend shopping or cooking, and the energy you'll save. If you order over the phone, most things can be shipped to you overnight (for an additional cost, as well as an additional convenience), and delivered to you at your office. All you need to do is take it home, unwrap it, heat, and serve. There are many times in my busy life that this is just the ticket to simplified entertaining, and I know it is worth it.

There is an emanation from the heart in genuine hospitality which cannot be described but is immediately felt, and puts the stranger at once at his ease.

Washington Irving

Menus

Knowing how to put different food items together in a menu is a talent in itself, but with all of the many ways to purchase food these days, it is getting easier. Here's a menu that I have used when I know I am having company later in the week but won't have time that day to prepare. Most of these things are "make-ahead" or store-bought, and you can still feel confident serving up a delicious, healthy meal.

Make-Ahead Menu

Hors d'oeuvres

Marinated Brussels sprouts*
Ginger dip* for carrot sticks, snow peas,
and cherry tomatoes

Main course

Chicken and mushroom bake*
Rice pilaf (boxed)
Steamed green beans with chopped onion
Dinner rolls served with apple butter

Dessert

Cup custard * (see page 90)

*recipe included

Marinated Brussels Sprouts

This recipe keeps very well in a covered container in the refrigerator.

1 bag frozen Brussels sprouts	2–3 tablespoons chopped parsley
½ cup tarragon vinegar	1 tablespoon sugar
½ cup vegetable oil	1 clove garlic, minced
2–3 tablespoons chopped scallions	1 teaspoon salt

Cook Brussels sprouts in boiling water for 5 minutes, drain. Mix together the remaining ingredients and add to the cooked Brussels sprouts. Put in covered container and chill overnight. Serve cold with toothpicks.

Ginger Dip

1 cup mayonnaise	2 teaspoons grated onion
4 tablespoons soy sauce	1 teaspoon cider vinegar
1 teaspoon ground ginger	

Mix all of the ingredients together. Add 2 tablespoons of milk if the dip is too thick. Cover and chill until ready to serve with raw vegetables.

Chicken and Mushroom Bake

6 whole chicken breasts, skinned, boned, and halved	1 ½ cups sliced mushrooms
1 can cream of mushroom soup	1 cup sour cream
	1 cup dry white wine
	2 teaspoons dried basil

Arrange chicken breasts in a shallow 9 x 13 baking dish. Mix all other ingredients together in bowl. Pour over chicken breasts. Sprinkle with freshly ground pepper. Bake in a 350°F oven for one hour or until chicken is browned and cooked through. Can be made the day before and reheated.

Cooking Shortcuts

Don't think you have to do it all yourself! Let your guests cook after they arrive. Plan your menu so that things can be made by everyone who is there. Have someone chop the vegetables for the salad while sitting at the counter enjoying a beer or glass of wine. Let someone else make the garlic bread. Get help with the grilling. Feel comfortable giving some assignments. People love to get involved.

~

Wash and dry all your lettuce when you bring it home from the supermarket. Then you have the beginnings of a salad all ready to go, saving you time later.

~

Don't hesitate to use jarred sauces for quick desserts. They can dress up plain cake, ice cream, or frozen yogurt, and can be chocolate, butterscotch, or fruit based. Lemon curd is wonderful on fresh berries, for instance; add a cookie and you have a special sweet treat.

~

People love to customize their meals, and this can save you from having to prepare all of the food by yourself. For example, for fun sandwiches that people can make themselves, use wraps like pita bread, tortillas, and taco shells. These help turn an ordinary sandwich into a party sandwich in an instant.

FUN SANDWICH IDEAS

Turkey and Swiss Roll-Ups:
Take sliced turkey, sprouts, and Swiss cheese. Lay them on a flour tortilla that has been spread with honey mustard. Roll up several and place them on a plate; microwave on high for 1 minute, until the cheese is melted. Serve with chips and a pickle for a quick, warm lunch.

Veggie Tacos:
Fill a crisp taco shell with a combination of any of the following: sliced avocados, salsa, sour cream, fresh-cooked corn kernels, chopped red and green peppers, diced cucumbers, chopped onions, grated carrots, and sprouts. Top with grated jack cheese, and sprinkle with fresh cilantro, oregano, or basil. Try any combination you like!

There are some wonderful and easy boxed mixes in grocery stores for foods that are delicious and certainly good enough for company. Some of the flavored rice pilaf, couscous, and rice and bean mixes, for instance, make nice side dishes with practically no fuss.

Fresh bread always adds a wonderful touch to a meal, and the quick-bread mixes that call for a can of beer or club soda are terrific. A wide variety of choices can usually be found in any grocery store.

Use a Crock-Pot! One-pot meals are easy and can be a lifesaver for weekday dinner parties. Just place the ingredients for your dish in the pot in the morning and let them cook all day. If the crowd warrants, get two pots simmering. Some recommendations are chicken, chili, and stew-type dishes. This will save you enormous amounts of dinner-preparation time right after work. Just put together a salad, warm up the bread, and your meal is complete.

Fruit Crisp Topping

Blend together a large batch of topping for an apple crisp and keep it in the freezer. If you divide it into smaller quantities before you freeze, it you can use it as needed.

4 cups rolled oats
I cup granola
2 cups chopped walnuts or pecans
2 cups brown sugar
½ cup flour
2 tablespoons cinnamon
I teaspoon nutmeg
I½ cups butter

Blend all ingredients together until crumbly. Store in four zipper-locked bags in your freezer until ready to use. To prepare crisps, peel, core, and slice apples, pears, peaches, or other fruit to fill a greased 8 X 8 glass pan. Sprinkle the topping from one bag over the fruit and bake at 350°F until the fruit is tender and the crisp is browned.

MAKES 4 CRISPS

If you are not fond of Crock-Pots or do not have one available, prepare a casserole to cook a day ahead of time. To make it a one-dish meal, make sure to add plenty of vegetables.

Use the weekend, when you have more time, to make something like a pot roast or stew before a midweek dinner party and freeze it. This type of meal usually tastes better on the second or third day, anyway, since the flavors get to mingle more.

When you don't have too many guests at once, prepare attractive dinner plates for everyone in the kitchen, then take them to the table. This way you can cut down on the number of serving dishes and utensils you will have to clean up afterward, and you'll never wonder if you'll have enough, since you are serving the portions yourself.

Plan a "bring-your-own-toppings" pizza party. You provide the crusts and let everyone help construct the pizzas by adding vegetables, sausages, and so on. Try this with tacos and sundaes, too.

Better yet, have pizza delivered for your party! Start out with a glass of juice, soda, wine, or beer and some nice hors d'oeuvres. Let guests pick their own pizza, and then time the delivery so that the doorbell rings when you are ready to eat.

Pick up a premade vegetable or fruit tray at the market on your way home from work. These are usually available fresh every day, but if you like, call ahead of time to be sure yours is ready. This will save you from having to shop for the groceries and spending time cleaning and slicing the produce.

~

Before hosting weekend guests, cook several days' meals ahead when you have more time. This way, when your guests arrive, the main part of each meal is already cooked and in the refrigerator or freezer.

~

Use large, heavy-duty zipper-locked bags for freezer storage of things such as bagels and muffins. You can easily pull out a few at a time, or even add a few at a time, and this way all of the bagels or muffins stay together instead of getting lost in the crush.

~

Go potluck as often as possible. Most people like making their special dish; if not, they'll bring store-bought rolls or chips. If you have a lot of people coming to your party, don't worry about assigning dishes. It almost always works out to a balanced meal. Even if everyone does bring a salad, they'll probably all be delicious and low fat, and people will still be happy. Remember, most people make something they like to eat, so it has to be good.

Homemade Pesto

This pesto is easy to make and keeps well in the refrigerator for a couple of months, or in the freezer for a year.

⅓ cup plus 1 tablespoon olive oil
1 cup chopped fresh basil leaves
½ cup pine nuts
3 cloves garlic, minced
⅔ cup grated Parmesan cheese
Salt and pepper

Combine ⅓ cup olive oil with the remaining ingredients and process it in your food processor or blender to make a thick paste. Transfer the pesto to a container and smooth out the top, covering with a thin coating of extra olive oil. If you wish, freeze smaller portions in ice cube trays and cover with plastic wrap. Pop out individual cubes as needed.

During the holidays one year, I bought a large, fresh, hot vegetable lasagna from a local Italian restaurant. I knew it would be too much for my family, so before I served it, I took out smaller "dinner-for-two" portions and put them in microwaveable pans for freezing. I was able to pull them out whenever I needed them with little or no effort. Be sure to label everything you freeze so that you can guarantee freshness and remind yourself of what you have already prepared.

Make only one dish from scratch and buy the rest. For the one you make yourself, choose something simple that you are familiar with, perhaps a lasagna that calls for sauce from a jar, and build the rest of the menu around it. Buy everything else already prepared, and say yes to any guests who offer to contribute food.

~

Don't forget to make extras the next time you're in the cooking mode. My mother always makes three or four pies at once, even though she lives alone. She did so when our family was big, and even now she would rather keep several pies "ready to go" in the freezer than make extra messes to clean up. This simplifies her entertaining immediately.

~

If you have children who nap, pick one day of the month and forget about the daily laundry, dishes, and clutter. Instead, use the nap time to make a terrific, freezable party dish that you can store away and simply pull out and use for a spontaneous occasion.

JUST REHEAT

To help you enjoy your own party, try to choose menu items that you can make ahead. A quick warm-up in the oven is okay, but don't choose items that need to be prepared just prior to serving.

Try to make your main dishes ahead of time. Leave the more simple salads, appetizers, and desserts for the day of the party, and let your kids help make these items. During the party, give credit to your child; refer to "Tommy's brownies" or "Sara's salad" and let the child help serve the guests as well. Giving credit will win smiles from your children, and encourage them to help again next time.

Kitchen Staples

Keep a cupboard reserved (and known as "hands off") for snacks, special treats, or hors d'oeuvres to serve to any spur-of-the-moment guests. You can be as creative as you like with your staples, and really surprise your guests. My mother used her most creative juices once when my dad brought home unannounced company. She served Ritz crackers spread with peanut butter, a dollop of ketchup, and chopped onions. They were truly a big surprise, and a big hit!

Always keep on hand the ingredients for one simple meal that most people enjoy, and that you like to make. Avoid serving this meal to your family on a regular basis, so that you will not become bored with it. Remember to replace the meal ingredients each time so that spur-of-the-moment guests don't throw you.

MUST-HAVE-ON-HAND ITEMS

My pantry always has the following items. I am sure you have some "must-haves" of your own:

Baking staples:
Flour, sugar, chocolate chips, vanilla, brown sugar, baking soda, baking powder, powdered sugar, raisins, cocoa, cake mixes, corn oil, honey, herbs, and spices. (All of the ingredients for baking chocolate chip cookies!)

Snacks:
Popcorn, mixed nuts, chips, salsa, peanut butter, jelly, pizza sauce, crackers, cheeses, olives, and pickles.

Hors d'oeuvres:
Canned chickpeas, smoked oysters, sun-dried tomato spread, olive paste, canned salmon, chutneys, jams, cream cheese, and Parmesan cheese.

Odds and ends:
Maple syrup, canned fruit, gelatin, fudge sauce, balsamic vinegar, sesame oil, specialty rices, white rice, pasta, pasta sauce, barbecue sauce, soup mixes, canned soup, macaroni and cheese mix, and olive oil.

Beverages:
Decaf and regular coffee, herbal teas, cocoa, juices, soda, sparkling waters, beer, red and white wine, and assorted liquors.

Freezer:
Frozen peas, spinach, cheese tortellini, homemade pesto, boneless chicken breasts, berries, frozen juices, ice cream, and frozen yogurt.

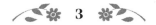

3

Entertaining at Home

When it comes to entertaining at home, I learned everything I know from my mother. She throws great planned parties, is never at a loss when more people show up for dinner than she expected, and is entirely sincere and honest in her requests to "stop by if you're in the area." Nothing fazes her, she never seems ruffled, and her food is fantastic!

But what I have come to love and appreciate most is that she truly enjoys making people happy, herself included. As she entertains, she gives the illusion of simplicity — and I think that that is half the battle. If you can pretend that what you are doing is simple, then the action itself may become simple. It's certainly worth a try!

While some of the ideas in this book suggest how to play host somewhere other than where you live (see chapter 10 in particular), there are many advantages to entertaining at home. You know what tasks need to be done, how cluttered the den is, and how much longer the chicken needs to roast. You are in control of the situation and can handle anything else as it comes up. You are on your own home court, so to speak, and therefore should have the home court advantage.

But adding to the challenge of this equation is that it *is* your home, where you and your family live, and it can sometimes seem an insurmountable obstacle to entertaining. The semipermanent piles, the clutter, the dirty bathrooms, the rugs. Even if you love to cook and set up for a party, you need a clean surface to work on!

So as you get ready for a party or an evening of entertaining, put yourself in your guests' shoes. Or think back to the last time you were at a friend's house for an event. What do you remember about the get-together? Was it the dust on the mantel or the fantastic fudge sauce served over ice cream? What sparked your conversation — the books stacked in a corner of the living room or the new family photos of their trip to the Adirondacks? Were you angry when you had to peek under their bathroom cabinet to find a new roll of toilet paper, or did you laugh at the thought of doing the very same thing at your own house that morning?

Other people are much more forgiving and tolerant of our imperfections than many of us are ourselves. While some of the above examples of imperfection may seem comical, be prepared for any or all of them to happen in your own home. And if one does, remember, it's not the end of the world. You may even inspire others who are uncomfortable about entertaining to do so themselves one of these days!

Home Preparation

Don't worry if your house or apartment isn't just right, or isn't gleaming, larger, or better equipped. People love to simply get together. Your true friends will not judge you on your housekeeping skills.

Do as much as possible in advance. I set the table the day before or the morning of a party. So even if I am running behind in the kitchen, my guests still know that I expected them, and a meal is forthcoming. This way, your table will also end up looking more beautiful than if you'd rushed to set it as guests were arriving.

~

Pull out your most special dishes and serving items. This will help create a beautiful setting.

SCENTS

Be sure to light your scented candles and start your potpourri simmering before your guests arrive. This gives your home time to really start to smell great.

Candles provide a festive, elegant, cozy, or romantic atmosphere. They come in hundreds of sizes and shapes, are long lasting, are economical, and change the mood instantly.

~

There are lots of other ways to make your house smell good when people come in, too. You can roast a chicken with lemon and herbs, make brownies, mull cider, or simply boil some water with cinnamon sticks and sliced oranges. That's something they'll remember.

Don't neglect the outside entrance to your home as you spruce up inside. Have a seasonal accent at your front door: pumpkins, a basket of apples, wreaths, potted mums, or geraniums. And remember the front stoop. A quick sweep of the steps and a wipe of the glass door make a great first impression, and will save you extra cleanup inside after the party is over.

Don't forget to put some appropriate music on before the guests arrive. It does so much to set the mood for enjoyable conversation, and to distract the guests from the stray sock in the corner that escaped your notice.

Lay fires in all fireplaces in advance to dry the wood. Use starter sticks for easy lighting when the guests do arrive, to avoid taking time away from them. Look into the new, enhanced gas-log fireplaces. They are clean, always start, and create a wonderfully warm atmosphere.

Firelight will not let you read stories, but it's warm and you won't see the dust on the floor.

Irish proverb

Prepare your music (CDs, tapes, and so on) in advance, and ask one of your kids to keep your selections going throughout the evening. Consider the tone you want to set (perhaps festive on arrival, mellow during the meal) and select the music accordingly.

If the party is outside, move the speakers over to an open window and turn up the volume. If you give your neighbors some advance notice, they don't seem to mind. Better yet, invite your neighbors so they can enjoy the fun, too!

Create different areas at your party for different types of people. Some like to dance, some like to talk, some need a distraction like a game, and of course, no matter what you do, everyone winds up in the kitchen.

For Large Parties

Have plenty of hangers on hand for coats, and empty the front hall closet. If you use your bedroom for coats, be sure that it is tidy.

If necessary, rent a couple of rolling coat racks. You can even keep these in your garage. This will free up space within your home, and, as the party draws to a close, the guests can pick up their coats on the way to their cars.

If lots of people will be arriving at once, create easy ingress to avoid creating a bottleneck with people standing outside for a long time. Get people into the flow quickly by suggesting, "There's a bar with wine, beer, and soft drinks in the next room. Go on in!"

~

Make parking easier by putting your own cars in the garage. You may need to hire a "traffic controller" or parking attendant to keep the parking situation under control.

~

For a very large party, alert the police department and all of your neighbors as a courtesy. The police will welcome the advance notice of increased traffic, and your neighbors will appreciate your thoughtfulness, particularly if guests don't park on their lawns.

~

Hire a piano player, a small group ensemble, or a disc jockey to keep the music going throughout the evening. Last summer, up in the Adirondacks, I heard of a local fiddler and asked him to play at a gathering at our home. "Only if I can bring my friends," he said. We wound up with a banjo and a harmonica, making for a great event. When the trio refused payment, we made a contribution to their favorite charity.

Throw up a tent! You can fit more people, you don't need to worry about the weather, the atmosphere will be instantly more festive, and you can even use it yourself for a few days if you want to really get your money's worth. The best of the tent suppliers do everything for you, right down to cleaning up the next day.

~

Ask your liquor store supplier to calculate your needs, based on the numbers you have invited and the age of the crowd, and ask him or her to deliver. Stores can provide the ice, mixers, and soda as well.

~

Hire a bartender and waitperson. They can clean up for you throughout the evening, leaving you time to be with your guests after dinner and little to do when your guests leave except go to bed. If this is too expensive, consider hiring teenagers or college students you know. They clean well and cost a lot less than an agency or individual in the cleaning business. They can also serve the food, watch the kids, and do the kitchen cleanup.

~

The easiest of all ways to host a large party is to have a caterer do the food, and it doesn't have to be expensive. Shop around. If you find someone whose work you like, you can use them again and again. Ask around for recommendations.

Have two bars set up so that people can spread out more quickly and not have to wait for a cocktail or soft drink. Bartenders are a great addition to the party, too, and need not be expensive. They help things move along more easily, and can also keep an eye on everyone's consumption.

~

Put the hors d'oeuvres in several different spots to keep the traffic flow even. Don't forget to tell people that "there is food in the living room and on the porch" so that they make the move and you aren't left with too much food.

~

Rent folding chairs to provide extra seating for your guests. This normally costs about $1 to $2 per seat, and is a real necessity for larger parties.

~

Rent dishes and utensils. It is quite inexpensive and cuts way down on your postparty cleanup since you put them back into their crates dirty.

~

Get a second refrigerator, with a freezer for extra ice, to save trips to the liquor store, and for bulky items. You can often find used models for much less at an appliance store or yard sale.

~

Push all of the large furniture against the walls to make more space if you have a small entertaining area.

Roll up your rugs and send your pets to a friend's house for the evening. No one will know they are missing! If your party is outside, keep the dog and cat in the garage. Nothing is less appealing than seeing an animal on the picnic table.

Cleaning Tips

Don't be too fastidious about how clean your house is. Too many people decide not to entertain for this reason. Remember, your friends love to get together, and they're more forgiving than you think. In fact, when things are too clean, people sometimes don't feel at ease.

~

Still, entertaining often ends up being a good excuse to clean up and get rid of all those piles in the living room. You'll feel better when the party's over because the house is much cleaner than before you "weeded out" and entertained; your family, too, will definitely notice the difference, and appreciate the effort.

~

Before actually cleaning your house, declutter. One easy way to do this quickly is to get some big boxes or plastic containers. Put clothes that are lying around in one, papers in another, books and magazines in another, and so on. (You can even throw dishes in one.) Hide the boxes in the garage, basement, laundry room, or somewhere else out of sight until the event is over.

If your "playroom" is also your living or family room, put some of the kids' toys away in bedrooms before your party so that the clutter is kept to a minimum.

~

Pick up before dinner guests arrive, but leave the real cleaning for after the party. For example, don't wash your floors before a large gathering. Instead, wait until the next morning. Then you can pick up all the dropped cracker crumbs and clean the floor at the same time.

~

When cleaning, stick to the essentials. Tidy, dust, and vacuum only those rooms that will be used, and clean the bathrooms. When a gathering emerges spontaneously at your house, the only rooms that absolutely must be clean are the bathrooms. The rest of the house will look good enough.

~

Keep fresh-smelling soaps in your bathrooms, as well as lightly scented potpourris or candles. Have clean hand towels available and a new roll of toilet tissue. Wipe down bathrooms with a sponge loaded with a fresh-scented cleanser. Include the floors.

~

If the party is at night, don't bother to dust behind or under things, but do watch for the spiderwebs on the ceiling that show when lamps are on.

Run all the dirty pots and pans through the dishwasher before people arrive. The kitchen will seem less cluttered as you serve the meal.

~

Clean the house the night before. Get all able bodies to do their share. For example, middle-size kids can dust and vacuum while you and your spouse tackle the fussier places like bathrooms and kitchen. Everyone should be responsible for picking up all of his or her own clutter first.

~

If your small children are "helping" with the cleaning, turn your vacuum cleaner into a dragon and give "dragon rides" as you clean. Also, invest in some child-size cleaning tools, brooms, or mops. Kids love to help, especially when they can do as you do. And it's never too early to teach them good habits.

~

If you have a formal dining room, use it. It needs only a quick dusting and a fresh centerpiece before the meal.

~

Consider using paper plates and plastic utensils for informal or large gatherings to save on cleanup time afterward. Keep plenty of garbage bags handy, and get someone to take them out to the garage frequently.

When you host a potluck dinner, have plastic bags ready for the dishes that people brought with them. Guests can take their own things home to wash, saving you time and precious kitchen counter space at the end of the evening.

Decorating

If you're worried about the white rug in the living room, either don't serve chocolate cake and tomato soup, or don't use that room. You want to enjoy your party, too, and not worry about who is walking where and with what!

~

If you don't feel your table is big enough for serving all your guests, put two card tables together and adorn them with a large tablecloth, using it as a buffet or as additional table space.

~

An easy way to add color, life, and beauty to your home is to place fresh flowers in a few vases throughout.

Nothing is really work unless you'd rather be doing something else.

Peter Pan

Add romance with lots of candles and mood music.

~

If you will be sitting at the table to dine, make sure the centerpiece is low enough to see over, and that the candles are in a safe spot. A good way to tell if the centerpiece is too tall is to measure its height with your elbow on the table and your hand pointed upward. If it is higher than this, remove it.

~

Your centerpiece should be fun, reflect the season, and be simple. Flowers are always beautiful, but a potted plant like a flowing philodendron or ivy can be just as lovely. If it is leggy, you can tuck some tapered candles in and among the vines, creating a nice effect.

~

Although daylilies earn their name by holding their bloom for only one day, they hold that freshness whether or not they're placed in water. For a simple, dramatically beautiful centerpiece, pile freshly cut daylily blossoms on a favorite tray or bowl. They'll last through the evening, though by morning they will be wilted.

~

Instead of using flowers as a centerpiece, put a nice bowl or pretty basket of peppers, citrus fruits, nuts, or apples on the table. It can be beautiful, and the food can certainly be eaten at another time. Or you can cut holes in food items and use them as your candleholders.

A word of caution: Do not use hot peppers in your centerpiece. We almost lost a guest one evening who insisted on nibbling some jalapeños.

~

Instead of flowers or fruits, use a collection you might have as your centerpiece. I have some corn-husk dolls, and I like to put them on the table at Thanksgiving. They face each of the place settings, and by adding some whole nuts, Indian corn, and pine boughs, I can set the mood for the harvest season.

TABLE DECORATIONS

Here are some fast, easy items to pile in a bowl as a centerpiece focal point, depending on the season:

Spring: Cut tulips displayed in a pitcher. Lily-of-the-valley at each place.

Summer: A big bowl of homegrown straw-berries. Fresh-cut herbs in a vase ... these smell wonderful as well as looking pretty.

Fall: Pinecones in a cut-glass bowl. Shiny apples in a big wooden bowl. Brilliant autumn leaves spread on the table. Indian corn and unusual gourds.

Winter: Pine or evergreen boughs interspersed with votive candles in holders. A bowl of shiny tree ornaments adds sparkle to any table.

*D*o have a fully stocked first-aid kit available, as well as a functioning fire extinguisher.

~

Don't feel you need to match all of your pieces of china, silver, and glassware. This is something only you will notice or care about. In fact, many restaurants mix and match patterns of dinnerware at the same table on purpose. It can help make dinner fun and more relaxed.

~

Try a tableless party. Spread blankets or tapestries on your dining room, living room, or family room floor (you might want to put a sheet of plastic down first to protect the floor from spills); push aside the furniture for lots of space; and stack piles of napkins in convenient locations. You have an indoor picnic that is simple, casual, festive, and fun! Be sure to serve your food on sturdy paper plates, use drinking glasses with lids and straws, and keep your menu simple as well.

~

Fresh flowers always add a bright spot on your table and around your home, but sometimes they can be expensive. Putting a single beautiful blossom in a dramatic tall vase can be just enough to set the mood. Even putting a single bud or blossom at each place at your table can be lovely and much less expensive.

Use pretty paper plates and matching napkins. There are beautiful ones available that aren't too expensive.

~

Collect baskets at garage sales and use all different shapes and sizes of them to hold all sorts of items: cut dipping vegetables, crackers, cheese, breads, napkins rolled up with silverware, jars of condiments. A grouping of different baskets helps create a beautiful table.

~

To roll your silverware up in linen napkins (perhaps for a dinner buffet), take the napkins and fold into a triangle with the point facing you. Lay the silverware across the point. Begin to roll the point around the silverware; halfway up, fold in the two sides neatly. Continue rolling until you have a nice, tight rolled-up napkin with silverware.

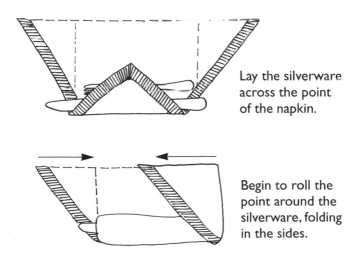

Lay the silverware across the point of the napkin.

Begin to roll the point around the silverware, folding in the sides.

Use interesting food items as dip bowls. For example, carved-out cabbages, bell peppers, round breads, mini pumpkins, round squashes, and fresh pineapples all make eye-catching displays.

~

When I have wineglasses set on the table, I take a colorful paper napkin, open it up, pinch the middle, and stick it with the point down into each glass. This instantly dresses up the table.

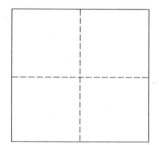

Unfold a large, colorful paper napkin.

Pinch the middle and lift up, forming a point that is gathered.

Turn upside down and place in an empty wineglass.

Entertaining
with Kids in Mind

When you're entertaining with kids, don't worry about making two separate and distinctive meals for the two generations in the group. Either make a meal that they will enjoy, too, or order a pizza for them.

~

If you are entertaining with your kids and those of friends, make the party time early. No one needs to worry about a baby-sitter, you have a few hours before the children melt down, and after everyone leaves, you still have a little of your own evening left.

~

Set up a scavenger hunt for the kids. Give each of the adults present one of the items on the list to carefully guard and dispense to the first scavenger. Be creative with your listed items:

- A special seasonal or holiday song
- A few stickers
- A shoelace from that person's shoe
- A hat to wear for the rest of the evening
- A few Legos made into some structure by the adult and the child
- A certificate for an extra-special dessert
- A video to watch when the hunt is complete

Kids can be pretty good if they are allowed to watch television in your bedroom and eat snacks on your bed. Be sure they wear pajamas, and throw extra pillows and snuggly blankets on the bed.

~

Young parents can form a group that meets at a different house each month (or even as often as each week). The host makes the meal for everyone, including all of the kids. Everyone enjoys a night out together. The more people in the group, the less often you have to cook, but the more you have to cook when it is your turn. The trick is to keep it simple.

~

If your children will be at your gathering, give them special jobs to do during the party. Give your daughter a disposable camera and let her be the "photographer" for the evening. Develop her pictures later, and let her add some to her scrapbook. Let your son be the official "appetizer server," or let all of your children be official "plate clearers" at the end of the meal. Not only will this be helpful, but it will make your children feel important.

~

After dinner, let the kids make their own desserts for a fun activity and treat. Try making sundaes, decorating cookies, or creating fruit kabobs using simple wooden skewers and bowls of cubed fruit.

Hire a couple of baby-sitters to supervise a kids' supper, including games and projects, while you enjoy your own adult dinner. Splitting the cost of the sitters saves everyone from having to find and pay for their own.

If you don't have small children but your guests do, keep a box of books and toys for them to play with. They needn't be new or fancy. Most kids enjoy playing with someone else's toys better than their own, no matter how old. Just be sure that the old toys are safe and age appropriate. You can also suggest that the parents bring a video or two that their children particularly enjoy watching, then let them do so during dinner.

Pull out the art supplies for your gathering of children while the adults eat. Stickers, glue, tape, scissors, construction paper, coloring books, and crayons enough for all will spark their creativity, and they'll have a ball.

Host a Sunday-morning pancake party with another family. Make up huge batch of pancake batter, juice, fruit, and coffee, and take special "pancake-shape orders" from the kids. This is fun, inexpensive, and a sure hit with children. They also tend to be "at their best" in the morning hours.

When hosting a dinner party that includes children, always make a pot of quick and easy macaroni and cheese. A child who may not like what's on the "adult menu" rarely passes up a bowl of cheesy macaroni.

~

Hire a baby-sitter to play with the kids outdoors while you clean for a couple of hours before your party. He or she can feed the kids early, making it more fun for them and for you.

~

When small children arrive for an evening party, make sure that there are a couple of places for them to snuggle up and go to sleep. They don't have the stamina to stay up much past their normal bedtime, and if your big bed has some extra pillows and a nice soft throw, they will be just fine.

Ask your child what he wants for dinner only if he is buying.

Fran Lebowitz

Entertaining around Food

Food is one of the simplest ways to focus your gathering and unify your guests. In some situations, merely opening a jar of salsa and a bag of chips makes it feel like a party. Although certainly not the only way to entertain, food is the most common denominator when it comes to entertaining. Food can help set the mood, fill in the quiet moments, and signal when the party is over. Yet your munchies don't have to be sensational to accomplish these things. Simple recipes, simple preparation, and simple presentation will make your life easier.

When it comes to food, make and serve what you like to cook and eat. Remember, it's your party! You will enjoy the preparation and the end product, and your guests will, too. What if you love to entertain but don't love to cook? Use the resources you have at hand to fill in the gaps. Have your guests bring specific dishes to help round out the meal. Order in part of the meal and make the rest yourself. Or hit the grocery

store and take advantage of the huge array of prepared foods that is out there. You'll be surprised
how the meaning of the word *homemade* can be
stretched.

People are instantly put at ease when they have
a drink (alcoholic or otherwise) in one hand and
something to nibble on in the other. Food is the
great equalizer — everyone has to figure out how
to eat that delicious melted Brie with warm cranberries and toasted almonds on top without making a mess. This chapter has tips to help you
simply plan, arrange, and prepare the food you
want to include in your party. If you love to
spend all day in the kitchen and have the time to
do so, then more power to you. But most of us
don't have the time or the energy to devote an
entire day to cooking for one event. And you
don't need to when you are entertaining simply.

Entertain around All of the Standard Meals

If hosting a dinner is complicated or stressful for
you, try a brunch, lunch, or breakfast. People
usually find such parties really fun and a nice
change, for the whole affair seems more carefree.
Don't even worry about serving the same thing
twice. If you love it, feel comfortable serving it,
and everyone raves about it, you've obviously got
a great thing going! On the other hand, don't be
afraid to experiment. You can always say, "I've
never made this before, but I wanted you guys to

A Warm Invitation

"One wintry day when my husband and I were at my parents' house for a long weekend, a group of our college friends dropped in to see if we wanted to go sledding. We had just had a huge snowstorm, the roads were closed, we had just gotten our electricity back, and this seemed like the only logical way to spend the afternoon. My mom yelled out to us as we headed up the driveway, sleds in hand, 'Make sure you come back for something to eat when you're done!' My husband and I were probably the only ones who took her seriously. My friends were thinking, 'There are probably 12 of us here, there's no way anyone can get to the grocery store in all this snow, and she surely hadn't known we were all coming.'

"But as our noses began to freeze and the shadows got longer, we all trudged back home to my house. And there, miraculously waiting for us, was a feast! Warm homemade soup, crunchy bread, chocolate brownies for dessert, and plenty of steaming tea and cocoa to drink. Nothing fancy, nothing unique, but the gesture spoke for itself. There was plenty of food, and the party continued from the sledding hill to the front of the fire. Food sets the mood, warms the heart and cheers the spirit — do you need more reasons to include it in your entertaining?"

Jennifer Gillis

be the first to try it." The following are some tips and menu suggestions to make every meal a successful, yet simple, event.

Breakfast and Brunch Ideas

If you have invited people for breakfast or brunch instead of dinner, you'll have the rest of the day to spend the way you want! Here are some good tips and recipes so that you don't have to get up two hours early to do it.

~

Pancake batter can be partially made ahead (keep the liquids separate from the dry ingredients), or just use one of the packaged mixes available in grocery stores. The recipe on the box is foolproof and fast.

~

Interesting garnishes and fruit salads can be made the day before. Some fruits (such as bananas) are better added at the last minute, though, to keep them fresh and prevent them from browning.

Events are sometimes the best calendars.

Benjamin Disraeli

A large griddle that covers two burners at once is great for feeding a crowd. Make some pancakes ahead of time, and keep them warm under a clean towel in a low oven. The microwave also works well for reheating pancakes and muffins.

~

To host a cereal bar, have an assortment of fresh-cut fruit and berries, five or six different kinds of boxed cereal, regular and skim milk, juice, and coffee, tea, and hot cocoa. You can even have a pot of oatmeal on the stove for people to serve themselves.

~

For brunch, use a buffet approach whenever possible, and go one step further by having people make their own. A breakfast cereal bar, a bagel and cream cheese bar, bloody Marys, mimosas (orange juice and champagne), pizzas, salads, sandwiches, chili, baked potatoes, smoothies, sundaes — have the ingredients on hand for any or all of these, then everyone is on his own.

MIMOSA

For each wineglass, fill ⅔ with chilled orange juice. Top with ⅓ chilled champagne and stir.

Here's a simple brunch menu. Everyone can bring different kinds of muffins, bagels, breads, and jams; you prepare an easy baked-egg casserole the night before, and bake it in the morning. Have a large thermos of coffee and hot water in the kettle, along with tea bags and instant cocoa packets, so that people can serve themselves. Serve several kinds of juice, and put fresh, whole fruits (apples, bananas, pears, peaches, plums, grapes) in a large bowl, rather than spending time peeling and slicing a fruit salad.

SINK OR SWIM

To test eggs for freshness, remember: Stale eggs float and fresh eggs sink.

Pam's Baked Eggs

12 eggs, slightly beaten
1 cup milk
1 teaspoon dry mustard
1 teaspoon instant minced onion
2 cups chopped ham
2 cups cheddar, grated
Salt and pepper to taste

Beat into the eggs the milk, mustard, and onion. Add ham, cheese, and seasonings. Pour into a greased 9 x 13 glass pan. Bake in a 350°F oven for 30 to 35 minutes, or until it is puffed and a knife inserted in the center comes out clean.

8 SERVINGS

Quick and Easy Lunch Ideas

Order big sandwiches from a grocery store or deli, add some soup, chips, brownies, and drinks, and you have a party.

~

A big hit at one of my summer parties was a fresh fruit platter from the supermarket with vanilla yogurt as a dip. Add a tossed salad with several good bottled dressings to round out the menu.

~

Have a chili party. If you don't have time to make your own, call a local restaurant and ask the staff to prepare it for you. You can even take your own stewpot for them to make it in and no one will ever know that it isn't your own family recipe.

~

Winter gatherings are well suited for easy-to-prepare stews, chilies, and soups. Make them ahead of time, and you'll enjoy them as much as your guests will. Toppings can include shredded cheeses, sour cream, croutons, and minced herbs. Crusty breads make the perfect accompaniment.

Any intelligent fool can make things bigger, more complex. It takes a touch of genius — and a lot of courage — to move in the opposite direction.

E. F. Schumacher

Serve food that your guests make themselves. For example, buy pizza dough and divide it into smaller, personal-size pizzas. Supply some toppings and let your guests create their own. If you have a good barbecue, you can grill the toppings separately and then the dough, letting folks assemble their own. Very easy and very gourmet!

Caramelized Onions

1 large onion, thinly sliced
1 tablespoon olive oil
2 tablespoons sugar

Sauté the onion in olive oil and sugar over low heat for about 20 minutes or until soft, thickened, and translucent. Use on top of pizza.

GRILLED VEGETABLES FOR PIZZAS

- Small zucchini and summer squash sliced lengthwise
- Red and green pepper quarters
- Scallions with the green left on
- Eggplant cut into slices
- Onion slices
- Firm plum tomatoes, sliced in half

Brush vegetables with olive oil and sprinkle with dried basil or oregano. Place on a hot grill, brown on each side, turning once. Place in individual dishes for people to use as pizza toppings.

Make mini sandwiches out of small dinner rolls. Use chicken, tuna, ham, seafood, or egg salad as a filler. These look great piled high on a nice platter, and with an assortment of pickles and chips you've got a fun lunch for a crowd. Most people will eat two or three, but a hungry crowd might need more per person. You can make the salads the day ahead, or buy them in containers at the deli.

~

Summertime get-togethers are a breeze with fruit platters, chilled soups, cheeses, and smoked fish. Most summer soups can be prepared ahead of time, covered, and chilled.

Here is a gazpacho recipe that I just throw in the blender or food processor. It is different each time I make it, depending on what is fresh from the garden or market. This can obviously be made the day before — be creative and add your own special touch. The flavor is even better if you do.

Gazpacho

5–6 fresh tomatoes, cut in quarters	1 medium cucumber, cut in quarters
1 medium onion, cut in half	2 cups tomato juice
3 cloves fresh garlic	1 bunch fresh parsley
1 stalk celery	1 bunch fresh oregano
1 green pepper, seeded and cut in quarters	1 bunch fresh thyme
	Salt and pepper to taste

Put all ingredients in the blender or food processor and blend until smooth. Serve ice cold with a sprig of fresh oregano or thyme. For a nice garnish, add a teaspoon of sour cream or yogurt.

4–6 SERVINGS

Hors d'oeuvres

When serving hors d'oeuvres, a good rule of thumb for quantities is 8 pieces per person if you are also serving dinner, 12 pieces per person if you are only serving hors d'oeuvres.

Here are two delicious dips that couldn't be easier to make and can easily serve a small hungry party.

Claw-Lickin' Crab Dip

I 6 ounce can crabmeat
I 8 ounce package Neufchâtel cheese, softened
I teaspoon lemon juice
I teaspoon dried, minced onion
3 ounces sharp cheddar cheese, grated
Chopped parsley

Mix together the first 4 ingredients and place in a small, shallow baking dish. Top with cheese and sprinkle with parsley. Bake for 20 minutes in a 350°F oven, until the dip is warm and the cheese is melted. Serve with crackers.

Cup-a-Cup-a-Cup-a

This is a real favorite with most folks. The orange carrots look a bit like crabmeat.

I cup grated carrots
I cup mayonnaise
I cup Parmesan cheese

Mix all the ingredients together. Place in a small, ovenproof dish, and bake in a 350°F oven for about 20 minutes. The dip will get bubbly and browned. Serve with vegetable crudités and crackers.

Mix plain yogurt and strawberry jam and season with cinnamon and lemon rind. Serve as a dip for fresh fruit.

~

Always keep a bag of tortilla chips and salsa handy for quick and easy hors d'oeuvres.

~

For quick and delicious hors d'oeuvres, drain a can of quality salmon, place it in a bowl, top with a squeeze of lemon and a dollop of sour cream, then sprinkle with dill. Serve with crackers.

~

Create mini Reuben sandwiches by layering a piece of party rye or pumpernickel with a small slice of corned beef, a spoonful of sauerkraut, and a dollop of Thousand Island dressing. Top with a slice of Swiss cheese, and broil until the cheese melts.

~

Spread thin apple slices with liver pâté and top with a mini gherkin pickle.

GRATING CHEESE

Cheddar and other softer cheeses grate more easily if placed in the freezer for 10 to 20 minutes before grating.

Pour a favorite hot sauce, chutney, or preserve over cream cheese for an easy cheese spread, and serve with crackers or mini breads. I like to use pepper jelly, which makes a nice contrast to the cream cheese.

BANANA IDEAS

For tasty banana chunks, dip in lemon juice, roll in a mayonnaise-curry mixture, and then in chopped peanuts.

Frozen banana chips are delicious, too. Just peel, slice, and freeze on a cookie sheet. Store in a zipper-locked bag until ready to eat.

Layered Dip

 ½ pound ground beef
 Taco seasoning
 1 15 ounce can refried beans
1½ cups cheddar cheese, grated
 2 small chopped tomatoes
 1 can black olives, pitted and sliced
 1 14 ounce jar salsa
 1 cup sour cream
 ½ cup scallions, diced

Brown the ground beef in a skillet, adding taco seasoning to taste. Mix in refried beans and heat through. In a clear glass bowl, layer the beef-and-beans mixture with the cheddar cheese, tomatoes, olives, salsa, sour cream, and scallions. Serve with tortilla or taco chips.

Dinner Ideas

Have people bring their own meat or chicken or kabobs for the grill. You provide the rest, but leave guests in charge of cooking their own meat dishes.

~

Have a fondue evening. Fondues can be involving and exciting. Everything can be precut by the butcher and placed on platters ahead of time; you just casually make your meal and chat for the rest of the evening. Try beef, shrimp, and chicken, with three or four special sauces, and serve a big green salad with lots of fresh vegetables in it. A crusty loaf of fresh bread is the only other thing you need. For dessert, serve fresh fruit, like strawberries, kiwi, bananas, pineapple chunks, or large grapes, and cubed angel food cake for dipping into a chocolate fondue.

FONDUE SAUCE IDEAS

Place small bowls of barbecue sauce, a mixture of sour cream and horseradish, some honey mustard, Russian dressing, and even plain ketchup at each end of the table, letting people put spoonfuls on their plates. Have extra cans of cooking oil or Sterno on hand, and an extra fondue pot just in case.

"Planned-overs"

These are a great way to stretch one meal into two or more. If you cook more than enough for one meal and plan on using the leftovers in a different way the next day, you have saved time in both preparation and shopping. For example, have a summer cookout of barbecued chicken breasts, corn on the cob, and potato salad. Cook more of everything than you need for dinner, and the next day, make a wonderful Chicken-Corn Chowder. This is particularly helpful when you have friends for the weekend and need to think through several meals, from Friday night to Sunday afternoon.

Use easy and inexpensive recipes that can be endlessly expanded depending on the size of your crowd. Ground beef with sloppy joe mix on noodles, spaghetti with meat sauce or pesto sauce with broccoli, and vegetarian lasagna are a few that come to mind. All of these can be supplemented with a big salad and garlic bread. For dessert, cookies and ice cream or sorbet are sure to please everyone! The choices are endless in the frozen dessert aisles in the grocery stores.

Strange to see how a good dinner and feasting reconciles everybody.

Samuel Pepys

Lemon-Herb Chicken Breast Dinner

Serve this chicken with corn-on-the-cob and potato salad.
Use leftovers to make chowder below.

6 whole chicken breasts,
    boneless and cut in half
Marinade:
  ½ cup olive oil
  6 cloves garlic, sliced
  ¼ cup fresh lemon juice

2 tablespoons *each* fresh
    rosemary, parsley, thyme,
    and sage
Lemon pepper

Marinate the chicken for 2 to 4 hours in the refrigerator, turning every half hour. Grill on a hot barbecue until done. Reserve 3 or 4 half breasts for the chowder recipe below.

Boil some corn on the cob, making sure you have at least 6 ears left for the chowder.

Boil enough potatoes for the potato salad, reserving at least 6 medium for the chowder.

6 SERVINGS

Chicken-Corn Chowder

2 large onions, chopped
3 tablespoons butter
3 tablespoons flour
8 cups chicken broth
    (fresh, canned, or cubes)
4 cups cooked corn
5 cups cooked chicken,
    cubed

4–5 cups diced boiled
    potatoes
2 cups cream, half-and-half,
    or milk
Salt and pepper, to taste
1 teaspoon *each* fresh
    rosemary, parsley, thyme,
    and sage

In a large soup pot, sauté the onions in butter until soft and translucent. Mix in flour and stir until well combined. Add chicken broth, heating thoroughly. Gently add corn, chicken, and potatoes and simmer (do not boil) for 5–10 minutes. Stir in cream, salt and pepper to taste, and herbs.

Serve chowder with a loaf of fresh bread and fresh fruit for a complete, healthy meal.

Another "planned-over" meal is boeuf bourguignon, served with brown rice after a meal of roast beef. This is a great winter treat. On Saturday evening, roast an extra-large boneless cut of beef, like tenderloin or sirloin, for your guests. You can rub it with herbs, stuff slices of garlic into tiny slits, and roast it until medium rare. Serve it with steamed broccoli, pan-fried potatoes and onions, and even Yorkshire Pudding (see recipe on page 83). The next day make the boeuf bourguignon as follows for a wonderful supper. People will rave and think you are a genius.

On the other hand, don't prepare too much food. A good casserole, a salad, and bread make an ample meal for anyone. Most people tend to overdo it.

FINDING SPACE WHILE YOU COOK

If you find that you are running out of oven space when it comes to heating up all of your food, use your gas grill to cook the meat entrée or to heat up pans of food.

Yorkshire Pudding

l cup milk
l cup flour
¼ teaspoon salt
2 eggs, room temperature

Preheat oven to 450°F. Mix the milk, flour, and salt together with a whisk. Add the eggs and whisk just until blended. In a 9 x 12 glass pan or 12 muffin cups, drizzle some of the pan drippings from the roast beef, covering the bottom of the pan. Pour the batter into the pan. If you are using muffin cups, fill them ⅓ full. Bake for 20 minutes, until puffy and browned. Gradually turn the oven temperature down to 350°F to avoid burning. Serve immediately.

Boeuf Bourguignon

l large onion, diced
4 tablespoons olive oil, divided
3 cups baby carrots
l tablespoon flour
l cup red wine
4 cups canned beef broth
Leftover beef, cut into bite-size cubes

2 tablespoons each fresh thyme, rosemary, parsley, and sage
Garlic salt and pepper to taste
½ pound mushrooms, sliced
Leftover potatoes and onions

Sauté the onion in 3 tablespoons of olive oil until translucent. Add baby carrots and sauté another 5 to 7 minutes. Sprinkle with flour and mix well. Add red wine and simmer, stirring well, until wine is slightly reduced. Add the broth and beef, herbs, garlic salt, and pepper, and simmer for 20 minutes, until carrots are cooked. Meanwhile, sauté the mushrooms in 1 tablespoon of olive oil until nicely browned. After the stew has cooked, add the mushrooms and leftover potatoes and onions and heat through. Serve in large soup bowls on top of brown rice.

6–8 SERVINGS

Cannelloni Shortcuts

Years ago, my husband, John, and I lived in Italy, and I was fortunate enough to apprentice in the kitchen of our landlady, Signora Trentini. The dish that we most loved was cannelloni with spinach. The secrets were homemade pasta and white sauce. When I first made it, it took the better part of a day, and I'd done all of the shopping for it the day before! It was quite an undertaking.

Now, after much practice and many years of cooking, I can make my own version of cannelloni in an hour or so. I try to keep most of the ingredients on hand, and when I want to prepare something I know will be delicious and special, I go to work. Sometimes I even take a shortcut by using sheets of pasta that I can buy fresh at a local market, preparing the dish like lasagna and thereby avoiding the tedious stuffing of the cannelloni tubes. This step alone saves an hour or more, and the taste is still delicious. People often ask for this dish by name when they are invited for dinner. In fact, I served it once to a party of eight, and one of my hungry guests ate an entire pan by himself. He shall remain nameless!

Lasagna is one of the most versatile meals around. It can be made with beef, pork, chicken, turkey, vegetables, or any combination of these. If you use jarred sauce, add extra herbs, mushrooms, sausage, or ground chicken, and bake it the night before. Then simply reheat at your leisure. Don't add mozzarella to the top until the very end of your reheating or it will harden.

Baked ham is a great choice to feed a crowd. Simply heat it up and glaze it. Spiral-cut hams are particularly nice, and come with their own serving stand. If you don't have a ready local source for these, there are many fine mail-order companies that specialize in these meat products.

Set up a unique salad bar for your meal. Restaurants aren't the only ones that can do this successfully! Guests can serve themselves exactly what they like from it, choosing their favorite dressing. The presentation will be beautiful what with all of the fresh ingredients on the counter. Save the leftovers in zipper-locked bags and make a gourmet lunch the next day.

Have a Thanksgiving-type meal for a special friend's dinner party. You make the turkey and ask each guest to bring an assigned side dish. This kind of meal isn't hard to make, and it's comforting no matter what the season.

Serve several kinds of pasta (rigatoni, shells, bow ties) with several kinds of sauces (meat, fresh tomato and basil, creamy red pepper, olive oil-lemon-garlic-herb) to make a wonderful spread. Add garlic bread and salads and let each person serve up his or her own creation from a buffet. This is inexpensive and easier than trying to time all of your dishes to be ready at the same time.

Pasta with Artichokes and Capers

1 large red onion, thinly sliced
¼ cup olive oil
2–3 8 ounce jars marinated artichoke hearts, drained and cut up
2 1 pound cans crushed tomatoes
1 tablespoon capers
Grated Parmesan cheese

Brown the onion slices in oil. Add the artichoke hearts, tomatoes, and capers. Simmer until you need it (at least 30 minutes) and pour over ziti, rotelli, or any chunky pasta. Serve with grated Parmesan cheese.

The ornament of a house are the friends who frequent it.

Ralph Waldo Emerson

Delicious Desserts

Have a dessert and coffee party. It's a little different, and everything can be prepared ahead. Pour the coffee, slice the cake, and enjoy!

~

For an easy, more "elegant" dessert, make a pan of brownies; as soon as they come out of the oven, place Thin Mints over the top. When these melt, drag a knife through the mints in a zigzag fashion. A nice design results, dressing up a plain brownie for company.

Oatmeal Krispies with Dried Cherries

2 cups shortening
2 cups brown sugar
2 cups white sugar
4 eggs
2 teaspons vanilla
3 cups flour

2 teaspoons baking soda
1 teaspoon salt
6 cups rolled oats
2 cups chopped nuts
2 cups dried cherries

Beat shortening, sugars, eggs, and vanilla together. Add flour, baking soda, and salt, mixing until well blended. Add oats, nuts, and cherries, stirring until all ingredients are combined. Place 3 heaping spoons of dough on a sheet of wax paper, rolling into a log. Repeat with the rest of dough. Place dough in a plastic bag and chill or freeze until ready to use. When ready to bake, slice into ½" rounds and bake at 350°F for 7 minutes or until brown.

12 DOZEN

Serve fruit and cheese for dessert. The dieters will appreciate the fruit, and those with hearty appetites can be appeased with good cheeses like Asiago, Gouda, Bel Paese, and even Gorgonzola or other blues. A nice selection stimulates curiosity and interest, and winds up pleasing every palate.

~

Instead of making a fattening dessert that takes up your time and adds inches to your waistline, put out a big bowl of fresh fruit and a plate of simple cookies. This presentation is simple yet elegantly healthy, and I am sure your guests will appreciate your thoughtfulness.

~

Make a double recipe of pie crust from scratch and split it among four pie plates, making four bottom crusts. Freeze them for quick quiche or crumb-topped pies. Throwaway pie plates work well.

~

Keep a store-bought pie in the freezer and pop it in the oven when no one is looking.

BAKING TIP

Dust raisins, chocolate chips, candied or dried fruit, and nuts with some of the flour specified in your recipe before adding to batter. This prevents them from sinking.

If you aren't particularly good at making your own pie crust, always keep the frozen kind on hand. Fill it with apples, blueberries, or your favorite pecan pie recipe and you'll have a winner.

~

Keep a frozen pound cake on hand and, for an easy dessert, make a quick sauce of frozen berries, sugar, a squeeze of lemon, a tiny bit of cornstarch, and a touch of liqueur. If the sauce is still warm, it will help thaw the pound cake.

~

Wintertime cocoa parties are fun, too. You only need the hot cocoa and a plate of cookies to cozy up with by the fire. If the adults want, serve some mulled cider or hot wine.

Hot Mocha Mix

This is great to have on hand for the winter months. Kids love to make it and everyone enjoys its soothing warmth.

1 cup unsweetened cocoa
2 cups sugar
2 cups nonfat dry milk powder

½ cup instant coffee crystals
1 vanilla bean, cut into quarters

Combine all ingredients in a large bowl. Stir until well blended. Pack into jars, being sure to have a piece of vanilla bean in each jar. Store in the refrigerator at least a week before using so that the vanilla flavor is absorbed.

To serve: Place 3 level teaspoons of the mocha mix into a cup. Add 6 ounces boiling water and stir. For an additional adult treat, add a splash of whiskey to the cup.

Cup Custard

One of the easiest and most delicious desserts is one that my mother-in-law shared with me. She knew that it would win my love's heart, and that it would become a favorite of my own family and friends. On a cold winter night I make a batch and serve it warm. It keeps well in the refrigerator for several days. It is quick, easy, healthy, and very satisfying!

1 can evaporated milk	1 teaspoon vanilla
Water	Nutmeg
4 eggs, beaten	¼ teaspoon salt
½ cup sugar	

Preheat oven to 350°F. Lightly grease 8 custard cups or small ramekins. Line a 9 x 13 pan with brown paper. Add enough water to the evaporated milk to make 3 cups. In a bowl beat milk, eggs, sugar, vanilla, nutmeg, and salt with a wire whisk. Pour into custard cups. Place cups in the paper-lined pan and fill the pan with ½ inch hot water. Add more nutmeg to top of each cup. Bake for 40 minutes or until a knife inserted comes out clean. Cool and serve at room temperature. Refrigerate leftovers.

8 SERVINGS

Peachie Treat

This is great alone or on French vanilla ice cream, cheesecake, shortcakes, and more!

Blanch and peel 4–6 fresh, fairly ripe peaches. Slice into a bowl.

Add 2–3 heaping tablespoons chopped fresh mint (save some leaves for garnish).

Add about ½ cup peach schnapps.

Toss gently, cover, and let sit in a cool spot for a few hours. Toss gently once or twice while it's sitting.

As an extra-special and unique item for your menu, ask each guest to bring an unusual fruit, already sliced or cubed. When they arrive, throw all the fruits into a bowl for an easy and delicious fruit salad. Add plain or vanilla yogurt mixed with brown sugar on the side, and you've got a terrific dessert.

~

Purchase a coffee carafe or thermos in which to store hot coffee so that you will always have two pots available. You can make a pot ahead of time this way as well. Putting one pot on the table is a nice way to let people help themselves. It also saves you from having to get up again.

Our life is frittered away by detail. Simplify, simplify, simplify.

Henry David Thoreau

5

Entertaining without Food

I f you just finished reading chapter 4, you might wonder why you would ever even consider hosting an event at which food was not the centerpiece. While not as common, there are plenty of entertaining situations that don't necessarily call for food as the major part of the plan. When you simplify your thinking and try to figure out why you are hosting an event, you may be surprised to find that serving your newest chili recipe is not a cause for the celebration. You may simply want to see a friend who drops in from out of town, cheer a family member who is down, or celebrate a promotion. All these things can be done spontaneously and quickly, and no one will expect a gigantic spread on his or her account. Munchies and soda are easy have on hand, easy to serve, and always appreciated — but even these aren't necessary.

You might even have more than a few friends who would appreciate not having to sit down for a meal. In this age of healthy lifestyles, stereotypical "party" food can be a major pitfall to folks carefully watching their diets. Instead, take the pressure of having to load up off them, and make your job as host much easier at the same time.

If food is not going to be a major part of your party, however, you will need another focus, of which there are plenty. Work together, sing together, garden, paint, or plan together, read together, exercise together, travel, shop, or decorate together. The possibilities are endless, but to a certain extent they must be planned in advance. If a bunch of friends shows up at your doorstep, you don't necessarily need to break out your "What We Can Do Together" list. But if you have invited people over and don't plan on serving anything substantial in the way of food, your guests should know this in advance, and you should have a game plan.

~

Have a craft party! Get together with a few of your friends and do something creative, like papermaking, candlemaking, soapmaking, or nature printing. Provide the materials at your house one month, and rotate the host and inspiration duties the next. It is always more fun to do things in a small group, and if you want you can even include the kids. They can work on their own modified project, and everyone can go home with a treasure to save or give, as well as a newfound talent.

Host a get-together to which all the guests bring a project that has been hanging over their heads. Some things are easier and a lot more fun to do when there is company — photo albums, ironing, garden planning, knitting, mending. This kind of gathering is especially good for mothers of young children, who never seem to get a moment to sit down and do all they want to do.

~

Have a gathering at which you place orders together to save money. This can be good for seeds for the garden, bulk foods, or even patio furniture. You'll often get a discount on shipping for larger orders, and folks can share items that need to be ordered in bulk.

~

Throw a murder mystery party. There are at least a dozen different kits for murder mystery parties that come complete with invitations specifying which character each guest will play, an audiotape of the murder background, and instructions for each character to open along the way to the solution. The focus here is on the game, which can last right through dinner.

~

Enjoy a sledding, snowshoeing, or cross-country skiing party with cocoa on a hill. Build a fire and pass the cocoa. There's no meal to cook, just good clean fun with friends.

Get some work done with good friends. Once a month plan a "work bee" with a predetermined group, each time at a different house. The host provides the drinks, the munchies, and whatever supplies are necessary for the project: wallpaper paste, brushes, paint, staple guns, hammer and nails. It's amazing what many hands can get done! Don't forget that you can bring the kids. Someone can entertain them while the others work. People seem to really enjoy working together, and those good feelings last a long time.

The test of pleasure is the memory it leaves behind.

Jean Paul Richter

6

Simply Sensational

I f you have made it this far in the book, then you are probably feeling ready to conquer a simply elegant evening. Remember, the meaning of words like *elegant, formal, gourmet,* or *fancy* is in the eye of the beholder. If you are used to having small children at your side (or on your lap) at dinner, then a peaceful meal among friends will be elegant. If grabbing takeout on your way home from work is a routine, then a roasted chicken and a homemade dessert will be gourmet. If your schedule is such that your family, without thinking, plops down in front of the TV and eats whatever they can piece together, then sitting down for a meal with cloth napkins and no sitcoms in the background will be fancy and formal. I am not saying that throwing a black-tie gala at your own home would be simple, but there are many simple ways to make an event more special.

For a few summers in a row, the need arose for a tent to be put up in our back yard. Two weddings, a family reunion, an all-inclusive company meeting and party — you name it, we hosted it. These were huge events that were not necessarily simple to plan or organize, but the minute the tent went up, a festive air came over the house, and indeed the entire neighborhood. It all became "an event," and we were eager to get on with the celebrating.

What we learned was that this was a relatively simple way to create a "party" atmosphere. And once the tent was up, we looked for other reasons to use it. We found that renting it for a week was only slightly more expensive than for a night, so we learned to plan a week's worth of events for "our" tent. Even just walking outside on a summer night with our coffee and enjoying it under the tent with its twinkling white lights became a special occasion. A tent-rental company can provide you with tables, chairs, linens, silverware, and glassware. You can also arrange for the rental company to set up and pick up after the party. You simply provide the space.

Unique candles, fancy napkins, a gorgeous bouquet of flowers, even balloons can also make a day seem extra special. Even baking a "party" food can set the mood. Last week I made some cupcakes for dessert and no one could believe there wasn't some hidden agenda or a birthday lurking right around the corner waiting to be celebrated.

Creating a sensational evening just takes a little extra ingenuity and planning; nothing need be elaborate or difficult. A good friend once planned a dinner around the summer solstice, the longest day of the year. She set up the event outside, with appetizers and drinks in the twilight, a grilled dinner from the barbecue, and dessert and coffee under the stars. The night was illuminated with votive candles and torches, so bugs were not a problem, and the effect was spectacular. There was nothing particularly "elegant" about the evening except the special mood my friend created for all of the guests. Learn to use your creativity, and your parties will always be simply sensational!

Embracing Spontaneity

At the other end of the spectrum from the "simply sensational" event is the quickly thrown-together event! Each has its time and place, and each can be a lot of fun. Being capable of spontaneity is not always easy, and some people are better at it than others, but I think it is something worth learning.

The true reason for entertaining should be that you enjoy spending time with your family and friends. The food, the atmosphere, the time, the decorations — all those things are secondary. And when an event is spontaneous, much is forgiven! There is no time to cook and clean to the nth degree. Instead, you are generously opening your home and your heart to those you love. And that is something important to remember . . . when you are entertaining family, friends, and neighbors, you are showing them you love them and enjoy their company. I'd take that gift over a perfect pie any day.

Being spontaneous is also about being flexible and rolling with the punches that are thrown when you entertain. If a spilled cup of soup is going to throw you for a loop, or not having the right number of cake forks leaves you reeling, then you may need to read this book twice! Both my mother and mother-in-law were great hosts, with their own distinctive styles. Elizabeth, my mother, is soft spoken, relaxed, and flexible. If another mouth arrives needing to be fed, she merely opens another jar of bread-and-butter pickles and invites that person to head out to her garden to pick a few more tomatoes. Nothing seems to rattle her, and you always feel comfortable as a guest in her home.

Helen, my mother-in-law was of the opposite nature. She was full of gusto and energy, and didn't seem to slow down long enough to be bothered by an extra guest. She would quickly get the party going by getting everyone involved in some activity or chore, and then bustle around them like a mother hen. She was almost a performer, and could engage anyone in conversation. One Thanksgiving, she burst through the swinging door from the kitchen to the dining room with a beautifully golden turkey, complete with all the trimmings, on a lovely silver tray. In her haste and general enthusiasm, she lost her balance, and the turkey came sliding off the plate practically into the laps of her guests! She quickly picked it up, never missing a beat, and turned back to the kitchen, saying, "Good thing I always cook two turkeys. Back in a second!" And sure enough, she did come back in a second — with the same turkey on the tray, cool, calm, and collected. She sat down to enjoy her own feast and never looked back.

Special Occasions

Get a bunch of helium balloons and you instantly have a celebration. As Winnie-the-Pooh said to Piglet, "There is nobody that can be uncheered with a balloon."

~

Have a box luncheon for a special occasion. Buy small cartons or food boxes and fill them with finger sandwiches, cookies, small bites of cheese, vegetable sticks, a piece of fruit, and a pretty napkin. Add a special peppermint treat. Tie with a pretty ribbon and all your guests can take a box and a hot cup of soup and eat on their laps. The preparation is all in advance, and the cleanup is a snap. Once my husband and I hired a bus and took everyone in our company for a special surprise event. Everyone had a boxed breakfast waiting and we had a great time eating on board. The trip seemed to be over in an instant.

~

Remember, lighted candles make every event seem special.

Be not forgetful to entertain strangers: for thereby some have entertained angels unawares.

Hebrews 13:2

Decorative ice cubes can be made by placing fresh berries, mint leaves, or mandarin oranges in ice cube trays and freezing them. Remove carefully by running briefly under cold water.

~

Make a roast for a special meal. It is always seen as elegant, it makes the house smell delicious, and, best of all, it is so easy as to be almost foolproof. Roast your vegetables with the meat, add fresh bread and a salad, and your meal is complete. What could be simpler?

~

For an anniversary party, try to keep the couple you are celebrating foremost in your mind. Will they feel more comfortable with a crowd or a few close friends? Is a splashy bash what they want, or a quiet dinner for six in front of the fire? Don't force it. If the party misses the point, everyone will be less satisfied.

~

Getting out the old photo albums is always a fun way to celebrate an anniversary and remember the good times. If you don't have time to put an album together, set up a couple of bulletin boards and pin up old photos, or just bring out the boxes of photos for people to browse through. This special activity lights up spirits and helps create a wonderful mood.

Don't forget to entertain your own family. They are truly the most important people in your life, and treating them to a special evening or celebration for no reason at all gets their attention fast. We have a red "You Are Special" plate that we put unexpectedly in front of a family member after a particular accomplishment, or just to give a well-timed boost.

~

Surprise your family with a very special meal. My mother used to do this each summer. When the weather was stifling, our appetites were lacking, and it was too hot to do anything, she'd bake a large, family-size shortbread for the six of us. Then she'd go out to the garden and pick several quarts of fresh strawberries, whip some real cream, and serve us the most outrageous strawberry shortcake for dinner. That's right, just strawberry shortcake and iced tea. Nothing else! We would eat and laugh and talk for a long time, and she would glow with pride knowing she had pleased and surprised us all.

~

Or simply have a "Sunday dinner" on Thursday night. If you can, try to linger over the meal in order to enjoy some family conversation, a small luxury that's rarely part of our busy lives these days.

~

Slow things down by serving fondue, where everyone has to cook his or her own meal at the table. It takes time and opens the door for some fun talk. Other "slow-pace" meals include steamed artichokes and dip (dozens of leaves to pull off and eat), as well as a lobster and clam bake.

~

At one of our daughters' wedding receptions, my husband secretly hired a skywriter, and while assembling everyone for a picture, at just the appointed hour, he pointed to the sky. There, two interlocking hearts were being created. Talk about a showstopper!

At another reception, one of our friends put on a minor fireworks exhibition with the help of a pro. We were surprised and astonished.

~

When company comes, and you would like to feel special, too, take everyone out to dinner. You can eat inexpensively at a Chinese or Mexican restaurant, or you can live it up and go for fine dining. Either way, everyone will have fun, including you.

Fancy and Elegant

Have a party for just part of a meal. Offer a couple of really special desserts, for instance, along with champagne, fresh strawberries dipped in chocolate, a fancy cookie, a puffy soufflé, a delicious chocolate torte, and special teas and coffees. This is elegant but not as much work as a full-scale dinner party.

Throw a formal "pull out your china and crystal" party. Splurge! Get a baby-sitter. Dress up in formal attire. Dust off your china, silver, and crystal. Prepare a gourmet meal that is still simple! Here is a wonderfully elegant menu that also makes things easy for the cook.

Menu

Hors d'oeuvres

Smoked oysters on crackers
Marinated mozzarella balls
Italian olives
(all from the deli at the grocery store)

Appetizer

Shrimp cocktail with hot sauce
(precooked and cleaned from the market)

Entrée

Pan-seared filet mignon with red wine sauce*
Fresh steamed asparagus with lemon butter
Broiled tomatoes with Parmesan and herbs*
*Mixed green salad with balsamic
vinaigrette**
Crusty sourdough bread

Dessert

Fresh mixed berries with sweetened sour cream*
*Top everything off with wine or coffee
and an after-dinner chocolate.*

*recipe included

Pan-Seared Filet Mignon
with Red Wine Sauce

1 tablespoon olive oil or butter
4 filet mignons, seasoned with garlic salt
  and fresh pepper
½ pound mushrooms cut in half
1 cup dry red wine

Heat olive oil or butter in a skillet. Add the filet mignons
and brown quickly on both sides. Add the mushrooms to
the pan and stir to coat all ingredients with the juices. Cook
for 5–10 minutes, or until the meat is cooked to your liking.
Remove meat and mushrooms from the pan and place on a
covered, heated plate. Turn up the heat slightly and add red
wine, scraping the pan and stirring until the sauce is
reduced by half. Pour sauce over the filets and serve.

Broiled Tomatoes

Slice tomatoes in half and sprinkle with garlic salt, 1 tablespoon Parmesan cheese, dried oregano or basil, and pepper.
Dot with butter and broil until bubbly and brown. (To save
time, prepare tomatoes ahead of time and broil just before
serving.)

Balsamic Vinaigrette

In a glass jar with a lid add ⅓ cup balsamic vinegar, 1
crushed clove garlic, 2 tablespoons water, and ⅔ cup olive
oil. Shake well before using. This dressing will keep in the
refrigerator for about a week.

Sweetened Sour Cream

Add 2 tablespoons brown sugar to 1 cup sour cream. Stir
and chill until ready to serve. This recipe tastes just like
cheesecake without all of the work!

Holidays

The holidays are wonderful, but as we all know, they can cause our stress levels to rise quickly. Of all the times to try to simplify, then, the holidays are it. One Thanksgiving, for instance, I hosted my in-laws for the week, as well as my husband's sister and her family of five for the actual feast. I had never cooked a turkey, but I was determined to do it with graceful expertise. With all the extra hands I'd have in the kitchen to help, I was confident that all would go smoothly.

And it did, until the electricity went out on Thanksgiving morning! Fortunately, I had made some dishes in advance and they just needed heating, which I felt I could manage somehow. But cooking a 22-pound stuffed turkey was going to be a challenge, and I knew it. My husband quickly suggested, "Let's do it on my new Weber grill!" I agreed, having no other alternative, while my mother-in-law secretly made dinner reservations at a local inn.

To make a long story short, we set a beautiful table; heated the green beans, mashed potatoes, and rolls in the fireplace using heavy-duty aluminum foil; grilled the butternut squash; and roasted that magnificent bird on the Weber in just three and a half hours. It was the most delicious turkey anyone had ever eaten! My mother-in-law was astounded and mightily impressed with our ingenuity.

Simple? Maybe not, but it would have been awful to have wasted that beautiful stuffed turkey. I think the moral here is: Roll with it. Sometimes doors close, and windows open.

Have your holiday party *after* the holidays. More people will be able to come, and they will probably appreciate the thoughtfulness of your not trying to cram in another gala event before the year runs out.

Put cranberries in the water of your clear vase before putting flowers in — instantly creating a festive holiday feeling.

One winter our family hosted sleigh rides pulled by large draft horses. We packed box picnics and passed hot cider. The snow was falling lightly, making it unforgettable.

Have a cookie swap before the holidays. Everyone brings four to five dozen of one type of cookie to the party and goes home with the same number of a wide variety. This saves all of you time, and inspires new recipe ideas for the following years. Be sure to ask each guest to bring note cards with the cookie recipe written on them to distribute.

Rather than serving hard liquor, which can be expensive, serve a simple bottle of champagne as a cocktail. It seems festive, and needn't be expensive.

~

Try a holiday secret Santa swap. Each child brings a gift for another child but doesn't put his or her own name on it. All the parents can bring a simple, homemade treat to pop into "stockings" (use a brown paper bag with the child's name on it) as well as an item for a potluck supper. Not much work for you, but loads of fun for everyone.

~

For a different kind of holiday party, have everyone bring a new gift and a nonperishable food item for a local shelter, wrapped and marked with the gender and age of the recipient. It is amazing to see the excitement and joy that people, particularly children, get out of giving at this time, rather than just receiving. Make arrangements with the shelter for delivery of the items. The staff will even be able to tell you in advance the ages, sizes, and genders of their clients.

~

Host a gingerbread-house-making party. If you don't want to bake your own gingerbread walls and roofs, use graham crackers, icing, and small milk cartons to construct mini houses simply, then decorate with a variety of candies. Serve simple hors d'oeuvres, hot mulled cider, and eggnog for the adults.

Individual Gingerbread House

1½ pint empty milk carton
4 whole graham crackers,
   broken evenly in half
Almost Buttercream Frosting
   (see recipe on page 110)

Assorted candies for
   decoration
Sturdy paper plates

1. Gently "glue" the squares of graham crackers to each of the four sides of the milk carton, using the frosting. Let dry a few minutes.

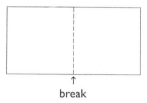

2. Form roof by "gluing" two more graham cracker squares to the carton. Make sure to use a small line of frosting at all edges so that the house holds together.

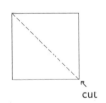

break

3. With a knife, cut a graham cracker square in half diagonally, using a gentle sawing motion. "Glue" these triangles onto the gabled ends, using a small line of frosting to secure. Let dry a few minutes to set.

cut

4. Frost the roof to look like snow, and apply candies for decoration. Attach candies to gingerbread house with spots of frosting.

5. Place on sturdy paper plate for easy transporting. You can even decorate the plate with cotton balls or coconut to resemble snow. Let your imagination take over.

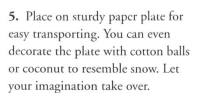

Almost Buttercream Frosting

½ cup white shortening
1 teaspoon vanilla
¼ teaspoon almond or coconut extract
3½ cups powdered confectioners' sugar
3–4 tablespoons milk or hot water

Beat shortening and flavorings for about one minute, then slowly add half of the sugar, mixing it in well. Add half of the milk or water and mix well. Gradually beat in the rest of the sugar and just enough milk or water to reach the desired consistency.

Have a Valentine-making party a week or so before Valentine's Day. You could make cards or cookies or both. However, I once tried to do both, and we never got to the cookies. I asked everyone to bring things from home to share for cards — fabric, glitter, pictures from magazines, glue guns, trinkets. People showed up with great ideas, and fabulous cards were made. Guests also got inspired to make cards together for friends they knew in common. Don't forget the red lipstick for kisses!

It's Halloween and friends are meeting at your house. Have each person contribute something: decorations, desserts, drinks, and so on. Ask one or two guests to come early and share the fun of decorating. Definitely have folks wear their costumes.

Host a Halloween hayride for families to enjoy together, then gather afterward for a simple supper such as take-out pizzas or subs, soup, and cookies and brownies brought by friends. Add hot mulled cider or hot chocolate to make it special.

Weekend Guests

You're entertaining "simply" with weekend guests. Your friends or family will be with you for several days and half a dozen meals. They usually want to know how they can help, and you should have a short list of things that would make your life easier ready when they ask. Don't be bashful. If they are staying in your home, they are close enough to help you out. Here are a few ideas for items your guests might bring:

A specialty food from their locale or region, like clam chowder from New England or Manhattan. If they bring enough, there's one day's lunch already prepared.

Fresh fruit in season and a breakfast specialty like muffins. Breakfast is the easiest meal to get on the table, but having someone else doing it sounds good to me, too!

SIMPLE GIFTS

If you are going to take a gift to the hosts of a party, think about what you might like to receive if you were entertaining. It might be something they can use that evening or at a future event, like a jar of special mustard that is great for dipping vegetables or cheese in as a quick hors d'oeuvre. Fancy olives, chutneys, or barbecue sauces are perfect gifts since they can be instantly opened and used in a variety of ways. Something you have made yourself is always special to give as well as receive. Wrapped in colorful tissue paper and tied with raffia or ribbon, none of these need be expensive. Here are some more ideas:

- A pretty scented candle to place in the guest bathroom
- A loaf of warm bread with the recipe tied on with a ribbon
- A bottle of wine or six-pack of special beer that would go with any meal
- After-dinner chocolates or peppermints
- A pound of special flavored coffee for after dinner
- A basket of herbal teas with soothing properties

- A small, unique kitchen tool that makes a process easier, like a lemon zester, a garlic roller, or a pretty cheese spreader; add the lemon, garlic, or cheese and the gift is truly unique

- A basket with new dish towels or napkins and a pair of pretty candles

- A packet of 5 to 10 of your favorite recipes tied with a ribbon

- A basket of scented herbal soaps

- A new paperback cookbook or novel that you've enjoyed

- Cut cookies, the recipe, and the cookie cutters all wrapped together

- A bottle of herbal vinegar that you have made or bought

- A bag of mixed nuts or dried fruit tied with a pretty ribbon that can be served that evening as a quick hors d'oeuvre

- A holiday guest book that you can sign at the end of the evening with comments about the fun you had

- A bag of dried vegetable pasta and a jar of special sauce for a fun and easy meal during the holidays

How about asking guests to bring a dessert for Saturday's dinner? Ask them to bring something that needn't be refrigerated. Refrigerator space will definitely be at a premium.

~

Beer or wine is always a nice thing to have on hand. If they bring it, they most likely will drink it, and not yours.

~

Munchies such as salsa, dips, cheeses, crackers, and nuts always work. It seems folks are always hanging around in the kitchen, and if there are nibbles available that they can easily prepare themselves, you are off the hook.

~

You could even ask them to bring some paper plates, cups, and napkins that would add some fun to the weekend. While you could always buy these yourself, they do add to the expense of the weekend, and you might feel more comfortable using them if your guests brought them as a gift.

~

Also, if they are going to be there for the whole weekend, go out for a meal or two. They might even help pick up the tab!

7

Enjoying Your Own Party

One of the best things about learning to entertain simply is that the time and energy you save can be filled with your own enjoyment of the event. Even those people who regularly strive to please others will find this appealing. Except for a very few high-tension entertaining situations that I can think of (enter taining your wife's boss or the estranged family members who drop in from out of town), you should begin every party by fully intending to enjoy yourself. This should not be a novel idea, but still, how do you do it?

Have you ever found yourself at the home of a friend who is obviously not enjoying himself? You can pick up those vibes pretty quickly, and if your host has had a tough time preparing, has disagreed about the evening with his family, or hasn't had anyone pitch in to help, the tension will be high from the start. You may find yourself wanting to lend a hand to make the evening run more smoothly. You might even feel like leaving a little early, just to put your host out of his misery.

To entertain should mean for all of us what the dictionary says: "to engage or enliven, absorb or occupy." Making your guests feel comfortable should be your primary job as the entertainer. Clarify your reasons for hosting an event in your mind. Do you want Uncle Tony to meet Becky? Do you want to thank your neighbors for being such good friends? Or do you simply want a chance to visit with your dearest friends, who you rarely get to see without children? All of these are great reasons for entertaining, but none has anything to do with a spotless home or an award-winning apple pie. Keep your priorities straight as you streamline and simplify your entertaining, and I guarantee that you, too, will automatically have more fun.

Remember that as the host, you set the tone for the gathering, whether you're aware of it or not! Even small children can pick up on your feelings, so try to take a deep breath as you open the door to greet your guests, and put any hassle that has been incurred as you planned your event out of your head. You certainly don't want your friends to feel they have "put you out" in order to pull off this dinner. The best parties seem to be those at which you can barely tell who your hosts for the evening are, for they are calm, happy, and enjoying themselves as much as everyone else. Strive to be one of these hosts!

Recently, there was a wedding in our family, and the bride and groom did a wonderful job making everyone feel at home at "their" party. They did this by mingling, chatting, dancing with family and friends as well as each other, and finding the time to have meaningful conversations with everyone who came to be part of this special event. It made everyone feel involved in the celebration and quickly set the tone for the evening.

The trick to enjoying your own party is to *plan* on enjoying it. You organized it, picked your favorite foods and friends, threw on your favorite CD, and opened your doors — now let the rest happen naturally. And who knows? You might find yourself having so much fun that you never want the party to end, and that an entertainer has been born in you!

Keys to Stress-Free Entertaining

People make the party, so be sure to plan on spending as much time with your guests as possible. If you are attentive, feel relaxed, and make everyone feel at home, the party will be a success.

~

Leave enough time before your guests arrive to take a nice hot shower or soaking herbal bath. Keeping your own stress level down will only help get things off on the right foot.

~

Don't dress to impress. Be yourself. Parties are pretty eclectic these days, and there is no such thing as being "over-" or "underdressed."

Dress comfortably, even if you are in formal attire. Nothing can cause more unnecessary stress than tight or ill-fitting clothing. You can become self-conscious and irritable pretty quickly.

~

Remember, simplicity is the key. If something can't be done simply, then ask yourself, "Is it necessary?" If it *is,* try to make sure it is something you enjoy doing. Then it won't seem like such a chore or cause more personal anxiety.

~

Give yourself as much of a break as possible by planning ahead. I can't say this too often. If it is an impromptu gathering, take the lead but go with the flow. No one will expect a perfect six-course meal.

~

Make your main course in advance so that you can enjoy your guests while they are visiting, rather than being stuck in the kitchen.

~

Open the wine and pour yourself a glass while you are preparing the meal for your party. Relax and enjoy the process!

~

Turn on your favorite music while you are preparing for the event. If it soothes your nerves or peps you up, it must be good.

SIMPLICITY VERSUS ENJOYMENT

Every year at the holidays, I make more than 20 dozen sticky buns as gifts to my family and friends for their Christmas-morning breakfasts. This is a long family tradition started by my mother-in-law more than 50 years ago, but simple it is not. At this busy time of year, I could much more easily buy something to give that would be lovely and enjoyed by all, I am sure, but here is the thing: I really enjoy making them! I enjoy the preparation of the dough, the kneading and pounding, the smell of the house as they bake, the wrapping with tissue and ribbon, and even the Christmas Eve delivering. Here simplicity isn't the issue. It is the pleasure I get from making and giving my sticky buns. Sometimes that's "simply" most important.

One year, there was a storm, and we were having a difficult time delivering the sticky buns. We decided to get up early Christmas morning and complete the job then. At 11 P.M. Christmas Eve, we received a phone call from a longtime recipient, saying, "Martha, if it would help, I'll come over with my plow and pick 'em up!"

Relax! Don't try to keep cleaning right up until the guests arrive. Make sure you have some time to catch your breath. People come to see you, not your house.

Try not to work too hard at your party. Prepare as much as you can, and if something needs doing at the party itself, ask a guest or two to help you. Or let it go. A big part of your job as host is to set the tone by having a fun, relaxing time yourself. Your guests definitely feel it if you are stressed out. If you're relaxed, though, your guests will feel relaxed, and they won't mind putting up with no dessert fork, or placing extra bowls of food on the floor when the table is full.

Learn the art of not caring. It's an important, difficult, but ultimately achievable attitude to cultivate. To help yourself get there, think of all the creative, wonderful people you know and admire who do not keep a squeaky-clean house. After all, what do you want to be remembered for, a tidy house or a generous spirit? Hosting a gathering is an act of generosity in and of itself. Say this again and again until you believe it!

A Helping Hand

Enlist the help of your family right from the start. Your well-being is truly important to them, and it only makes sense that they help you in a positive manner. Remember to return the favor.

Get help from a friend. Promise to return the favor, so you'll both be helping each other. I know someone who actually loved cleaning other people's houses and would do so in trade for baby-sitting, alterations, and baked goods.

~

Train your own help. If you do, you can always depend on things being done the way you like. And remember, if you are using teenagers, pay them well and they will become quite reliable.

~

Ask a friend or member of the family to throw the party with you. "Susan and her daughter Amy are hosting Thanksgiving dinner this year."

~

Entertain as a group by asking a few other friends to help. One can host, three can bring food, you can coordinate. Ask for help with the desserts from guests you are friendly with.

~

If guests ask to help with the dishes, let them! Besides saving time and finishing your work earlier, you can have some wonderful one-on-one conversations that might not otherwise take place.

~

For an "adults-only" party, call family members to ask them to take care of your children. If they are unavailable or too far away, get a movie that the kids will enjoy and set them up in the den or your bedroom with popcorn and drinks.

Give the noncooks cleanup duty, and then stay out of the kitchen and let them do it.

~

Create work areas away from your own space in the kitchen and enlist your guests as helpers. Plan

HOOP SOUP!

Each basketball season my family gets intensely involved in a longtime rivalry between our alma mater and another college. As the excitement grows, my responsibility is to host the pregame lunch, making sure that everyone is not only well fed, but out of the house in time to get the prime seats at center court. I always look forward to this event and try to prepare something nutritious, easy to eat, and hearty enough to hold us through both the women's *and* the men's game. Still, I want to be at the game too, so easy cleanup and preparation is a must.

This year I served three soups, made earlier in the week, put out lunch meat so that everyone could make his or her own sandwich, served big bowls of fresh fruit and platters of cookies, and I used paper plates, bowls, and napkins in the colors of our school. We all had fun, cleanup was easy, I saw both games, and most importantly, our team won!

ahead specifically how they might help: stir
the sauce, for instance, or make sure the bread
doesn't burn, fill the serving dishes with food,
chop vegetables for the stir-fry, and replenish the
hors d'oeuvres tray. Most people are very willing
to help.

Pregame Lunch

- Three soups: cream of tomato, three fish chowder, vegetable noodle
- Lunch meat platter: rolls of turkey, ham, lean salami, Swiss and provolone cheeses
- Cole slaw
- Small deli rolls, precut
- Chips, mustards, mayonnaise
- Apples and clementines
- Brownies, oatmeal krispies with dried cherries (recipe on page 87, white chocolate chunk cookies
- Beer, wine, soda, cider, and coffee

Hint: If you don't want *any* cooking at all, order the soup from the deli in quart containers, have the lunch meat platters made, and get the cookies from the bakery at the market. No one will ever know if you don't tell them!

8

Entertaining Small Children

Being the host to people who really appreciate a party is rewarding indeed! Organizing a party or get-together for small children doesn't take much work or much money and the smiles are worth every ounce of effort invested. Birthday parties are the most common reason for throwing a party for kids, but you can chase the clouds right out of a child's sky if you throw a beach party in January, a costume party for Halloween, or a secret Santa party around the holidays.

My daughter lives in a neighborhood that is teeming with children, all of whom follow an "open door" policy — if they can reach the doorknob, they consider themselves invited in! It is fun for the children, as they are never at a loss for playmates. A few weeks ago, my daughter and her son were making cupcakes; nobody was having a birthday, but they needed an activity and cooking is always a favorite distraction in their house. As the cupcakes began baking they watched as one then two then three kids followed their noses to their back door, let themselves in, and announced in typical kid fashion, "Why do you guys get to have a party?" Take advantage of the fact that a party can be as easy as opening a box of cake mix for this young and undiscerning crowd and celebrate often!

When you do plan a party for the younger generation, impromptu is fine but planning can make everything go more smoothly. Remember the ages of the kids, their limited "pleasantness" factor, and the attention spans that go along with their ages. Just don't expect too much and you will be all set! Food can be your centerpiece as it appeals to every age group and can instantly involve guests or divert attention, whatever seems appropriate at the time. Keep it simple, keep it fun, and you will all enjoy yourselves.

Finally, birthdays may not always be the joyous occasions that we as parents and caregivers set them up to be. Stay flexible, upbeat, and ready for anything when you are the host for children. And remember, a simple balloon can make a party as spectacular as a rented pony!

Young Kids and Birthdays

Most likely, if you have kids, you've thrown a birthday party or two. Even though your guests are far less discerning than any other crowd, you may have become frazzled beforehand as you thought, "How will I entertain these kids for the morning?" or "What kinds of activities should I plan?"

First and foremost, no matter what the age, your child may be able to help you plan the day. Who would she like to see on her special day? A good rule of thumb is not to exceed the number of your child's age as you plan your guest list. (If your child is turning three, for instance, have no more than three children at the party.) What would he like to do or where might he like to go? Keep in mind your child's strongest interests instead of worrying about pleasing everybody else. Also, try to make sure that your child gets plenty of rest before the party. Most tears come when children become overtired, and with all of the excitement of the celebration they will become tired more quickly. Keep it simple. Keep it safe. And most of all, keep it fun!

~

Young children's parties always come with parents included. Although you may feel you need to prepare a meal for them, keep the food simple. You'll need to devote your attention to the party, so don't plan a meal that will keep you tied up in the kitchen. Prepare your food ahead of time. Try a late-morning "brunch" party (before naptimes) with bowls of crackers, cheese, fruit salad, bagels or muffins, mini sandwiches, and, of course, cake and ice cream.

~

Serve mini pizzas on English muffins. These are a big hit with kids and work well on paper plates. Add some fruit and you've got a meal.

Instead of making a cake, make cupcakes, and decorate each one with a letter so that they all spell out "Happy Birthday _____." Cupcakes always say "party," kids love them, and they are a breeze to whip up.

~ ·

If you are having an outdoor summer party, use your picnic tables and serve a simple kids' menu. If you are grilling hot dogs and hamburgers, be sure to have a grill watcher at all times to avoid accidents. If you have a pool, it's the only activity you'll need. Just have plenty of extra lifeguards on duty at all times, even if it is just a small wading pool. Pool, presents, and picnics create the perfect summer party!

~ ·

Rent a pony for an outdoor pony-ride party. Kids love animals and enjoy the thrill of trying something new. This is a sure crowd pleaser.

~ ·

Throw a "tea party" and have fun with your child setting the stage. Set your child-size table with "fancy" linens, and have your child decorate place cards for his or her guests. Use fancy paper plates and dress the part. Cake and ice cream are all you need to serve. Play some traditional party games like pin the tail on the donkey and musical chairs.

Kids love to be read to. Choose an appropriate time during your party to gather the group and read a new and special "birthday book" that you've chosen for your child. Make this a tradition and try it every year, and, of course, add your own inscription as you add to your collection.

~

There are many places to throw your child's birthday party outside your home. Often, the food and entertainment will be all taken care of, so what could be simpler? Check your Yellow Pages and visit the party places in your area (playgrounds, roller-skating rinks, pizza parlors) before deciding on one.

~

Choose a trip to a museum, zoo, or special place as the main event. We took our son to the Boston Aquarium for his fourth birthday, accompanied by his best buddy, and then stopped at a pizza parlor for an easy meal. If you choose to dine out, call ahead to ask if they make birthday cakes, or if you can bring your own for the special occasion.

~

Throw a "color party." Send out invitations in your child's favorite color and call it a "purple party" (or whatever the color may be). Ask your guests to dress in purple, decorate your cake or cupcakes with purple frosting, buy purple balloons and plates and napkins, find some fun purple party favors, have some purple face paint ready. Pull out paper and purple markers, or purple paint and smocks if you're brave!

Winter birthday? Try sledding or pond skating for your child's party. Be sure to bring plenty of extra plastic sleds and warm clothes, and your entertainment is a breeze. Head back home for some hot chocolate and birthday cake, and build a fire in the fireplace to warm those toes and open presents by.

Or for another winter-birthday option, try holding a "beach party." Have guests wear summer clothes, and decorate the area with beach towels. Use beach balls for games, and pass out inexpensive kids' sunglasses. Decorate the cake with a beach scene, complete with paper drink umbrellas to represent beach umbrellas. You can even set up a plastic pool with games in it, but no water. To make this party even more summerlike, hold it at a facility with a pool, like the YMCA.

Throw a hiking birthday party. Meet at your favorite hiking trail with Baggies filled with homemade gorp (complete with M&Ms or chocolate chips) and set off on a nature walk. Hand each child a brown paper bag to fill with interesting natural treasures found along the way. Fall birthdays are a wonderful time of year for this, with leaves, seeds, and nuts plentiful. End your adventure with a picnic on blankets or at the trail's picnic area. Bag lunches are perfect for this party; serve Popsicles from your cooler in lieu of cake and ice cream. (Save the cake for your own family celebration.)

9

Entertaining Young Adults

As a mother with young kids who all grew up, I often found myself entertaining for my children's friends. Whether it was a birthday celebration, a pre-prom gathering, a graduation celebration, a sumrtime getaway at our lake house for our son and his college gang, or a group of camp leaders and staff spending an evening out at our place, these parties all had three things in common: They were always casual, we always needed lots of food, and they were always great fun.

My husband and I had the extra pleasure of sending our oldest daughter to college in our own hometown, and for four years were fortunate enough to have her group of friends gather regularly at our place for nights away from the cafeteria and dorm life. Although the quantity of food you will be preparing or serving may seem like a lot, the simplicity of these foods is the great equalizer.

Basically, young adults look forward to any kind of homemade meal, and "homemade" to them can mean pizza delivered to your home, cocktail weenies, or brownies from a box. It has always been a joy for us to entertain this way, most importantly because it has allowed us to make connections with the friends our children have chosen, and provide a safe place for our kids to congregate. Here are a few tips we have used along the way.

The High School Party

Do not serve alcohol. Have plenty of soda, juice, and punch available. Even if you trust your own child to have a beer under your guidance, never take it upon yourself to be responsible for other parents' children. The law is very unforgiving to those who serve minors.

If you are hosting a pre-prom or post-prom party, have fun with the "formality" of the event. Light some candles, pull out your good china, and make your kids feel truly special and catered to for an evening. Use luminarias in the driveway, decorate with pretty flowers or helium balloons, and dress up yourselves. By all means, if you own a tux, wear it! Pass simple hors d'oeuvres to your guests if you are the pre-prom destination: cheese and crackers, stuffed mushrooms, vegetables and dip, mini sandwiches.

Take lots of "formal" pictures, and make lots of copies. Your kids will feel terrific and will want to come back.

~

Stay away from messy food items, as the outfit is all-important to the high school student on this night! If you are the post-prom destination, food can be more casual. In fact, munchie-style will probably be appreciated the most.

~

Serve late-afternoon hors d'oeuvres and beverages, and make or order a cake celebrating a graduation. All can be made ahead so that you can truly enjoy this special day.

~

Again, pizzas will be a hit, but make them "mini" for a formal affair.

PIZZA IDEAS

- ◆ Caramelized onion and red pepper pizza (see recipe on page 74)
- ◆ Roasted garlic and sun-dried tomato pizza
- ◆ Pepperoni and turkey sausage pizza
- ◆ Goat cheese, pine nut, olive, and tomato pizza

Host a graduation party for your son or daughter, and, weather permitting, use the June outdoors to keep it simple.

~

Think about putting up a tent if you are worried about the weather, and use it for a week for other fun events. Try hosting this party with another parent to share the preparations and costs. We did this for our daughter and one of her close friends. Both of our families had similar invitation lists, so it worked out very well, and many of our close friends appreciated the simplicity of attending only one party instead of two.

~

Always have munchies, soda, and juice in your pantry for those spontaneous Friday- and Saturday-evening movie-viewing gatherings. Use your local pizza deliverer as well. What could be simpler?

~

Be sure to ask your children what is fun for them. Involve them and the party will feel like their own. They'll begin taking the initiative more readily in planning and preparing for the next one. You might be surprised: Our kids, for instance, loved making homemade ice cream in the summer and pressing cider in the fall. Both became big hits.

Designate one area as the "kids' entertaining room." If you have a basement or den set aside for this, your children will appreciate the privacy and choose your home as a safe place to have fun. Life is much simpler when they are under your own roof and you know where they are.

Equip the room with a television, VCR, and stereo system, if possible. Add extras like a pool or Ping-Pong table and a dartboard. If your basement is the place, keep your extra refrigerator there to save extra trips up and down the stairs. Self-sufficiency should be encouraged.

Host an "end-of-the-season" party for your child's team. Make a big pot of spaghetti or lasagna and share in the fun as they gather together to celebrate their wins and losses and camaraderie. This may be one of the highlights of the season, and it need not be difficult to throw together. If you can, gather some photographs of the season from other parents and put up a bulletin board for the kids to enjoy. Better yet, have a slide show, or show a videotape of one of their victories on the VCR. We had access to a computer for such a party, and were able to easily and inexpensively enlarge each player's photo into a giant poster. The team felt well celebrated.

For the group that still enjoys a good sleep-over, be prepared with plenty of videos, munchies, ice cream, and giggles. If your daughter wants to host a sleep-over, work with her on the menu planning and food shopping. Encourage responsibility and forethought, and let it be "her party." Let them stay up late in their own designated room, and serve a big pancake breakfast in the morning.

~

Most importantly, this time in your child's life will fly by. The more you are invited in to participate, the more both you and your child will benefit. Encouraging independence is important. Requiring responsibility is an absolute. Providing a happy, safe home is your job. Enjoy them and watch them soar!

The College Crew

One of the most important lessons I have learned is to always have plenty of food. Too much is better than too little in these situations.

~

Keep it casual. Casual dress, casual cleaning, casual buffet-style serving, casual seating (floors, laps, counters and stools, patios, picnic tables, lawns), and a casual time frame (come around six and leave whenever the party fades).

~

If you are serving to legal consumers, be sure to have plenty of beer available. Also, be sure to help establish designated drivers. Always have a few couches and blankets available for those who may choose to stay the night.

Keep an extra refrigerator in your garage or basement to help store the soda, beer, and extra food.

~

If you are into homebrewing, try setting up your own "keg-o-lator" by retrofitting an extra refrigerator. Keep it outside and the mess is never a problem. We invested in this system at our lake house, our son-in-law being an avid homebrewer. He always made a batch as he arrived at camp for the summer; the tap was flowing within two weeks. All you need on hand is a stack of cups. This system saves money and space, and really is simple once it's set up.

~

If you aren't a homebrewer, you can still set up a keg-o-lator in your extra refrigerator with a tap that's easily installed in the door. Keep it filled with keg beer from the store. You can get a commercial keg tap from most homebrew stores as well as many beer and soda distribution centers.

~

Keep freshly washed mugs or glasses in the freezer for that ice-cold, frosted look. A frosted glass will keep your beverages icy cold and make any drink seem more special, even lemonade.

~

Because of the casual style of your dinner, be sure to have plenty of munchies for the predinner crew. Chips and salsa, bowls of popcorn and pretzels, veggies and dips, hot chicken wings (available in bulk at your grocery store), "pigs in a blanket" (hot dogs wrapped in biscuits), meatballs served with toothpicks, cheese and crackers, bowls of grapes, and mini pizzas are a few of my favorite ideas. All are simple to find, prepare, and serve. Many grocery store deli sections can make large amounts of meatballs, sliced vegetable trays, and other accompaniments to save you time and effort as well.

~

Have a fun activity planned for those who are interested. We created a mini nine-hole golf course at our summer place. We keep a sign-in book for our guest golfers and see how well we all stack up! Croquet, horseshoes, boccie, Frisbee, volleyball, badminton, Wiffle ball, and even pick-up hoops and foul-shooting contests in the driveway are always fun.

~

Play lots of great music throughout the evening. Set up your speakers so that the music can be heard in various rooms (or outdoors, if that is where you are entertaining) and have your selections prepared before the evening begins. Feel free to invite your guests to bring their own CDs or cassettes in from their cars as well.

On one impromptu summer evening, four of our son's pals arrived, each with a car full of friends. They pulled all of the cars up to the volleyball court, left the lights and car radios on (to the same station, gratefully), and played volleyball under the stars for two hours.

Your meal need not be extravagant, but again, be sure to have plenty. We've found barbecued chicken, pizza, lasagna, spaghetti and meatballs, meat and vegetable kabobs, and large stews to be great main courses. Add salad, plenty of garlic bread, and a serve-yourself dessert counter (cookies, brownies, ice cream with toppings), and you've got a simple, delicious meal that usually appeals to most in the crowd.

~

If you have a pool and you are entertaining in the summertime, open it up for evening dips. First and foremost, be safe: Have a lifeguard on duty at all times. Moonlight swimming ends many of our summer events, hand in hand with coffee or hot chocolate under the stars.

~

If you have a garden, involve your guests in harvesting the lettuce for the salad. People rarely mind being put to work, and are often enlightened to their own delight as they learn how to pick a head of lettuce or dig a hill of potatoes. We have had fun sending guests out for "pick whatever you like from the garden" assignments, then preparing the food as a group and eating a vegetable smorgasbord.

~

Try hosting a party at a unique spot on your property. We often entertain by our "Council Ring" campfire — it's at the edge of our property, by our hayfield. Two picnic tables and plenty of garden carts help set the stage. Have the kids pitch in by pulling the food and drinks from the front door out to the tables in the carts. Many hands make light work, and this ends up being a fun excursion. Have extra sweatshirts on hand as the night gets chilly, and extend your dinner into the roasting of marshmallows and S'more making (graham crackers, roasted marshmallows, and chocolate bars made into a sandwich). Something about a campfire makes an evening special. We've had friends write to tell us, "We don't want to wash the sweatshirts. The smoky aroma reminds us of that great evening together!"

For an extra-special event, hire a DJ or band. Second to good food, nothing is appreciated more by this age group than good music. Let loose and join the dance floor — you'll enjoy the party yourself for sure!

If there is someone in the group with talent, ask him or her to sing, play the guitar, or just entertain. When kids get going in their own style, it is wonderful!

If you have a deck, put it to use. This is the perfect outdoor spot for eating, talking, relaxing, and later, watching the stars. In the summer, we pull futons and sleeping bags onto the deck or out to the backyard to stretch out and enjoy the northern lights with a cool drink in hand.

Ask for your children's involvement and suggestions. What would they enjoy doing, eating, listening to, drinking? Most likely, they will be the best judges of all of these matters if it is *their* friends being entertained.

~

Unlike some adult events, you can involve your pets, particularly in the summer. Kids love them, and somehow your golden retriever seems to fit much better into this crowd than in your adult dinner-party scenario.

~

Offer a door prize. Pick a totally random requirement for the winner (someone wearing red high tops, or the guest who lives the farthest away), and watch the surprise as you hand over a totally random prize (a gag T-shirt or hat) as the evening unfolds.

Manifest plainness,
Embrace simplicity,
Reduce selfishness,
Have few desires.

Lao-tzu

10

Entertaining Elsewhere

One of the best ways to ease into entertaining, or to take a break from entertaining in your own home, is to host a gathering of people elsewhere. "Is this allowed?" you might find yourself asking, or "I've never even thought of that!" you might be saying with delight. This is a very simple way to get a group of people together in an informal style and with minimal effort for you. Another benefit of hosting an event somewhere other than your home is that you can have bigger crowds and split up the responsibilities. You'll get all the enjoyment with only half the effort!

I was talking with one of our young friends, who recently moved to Manchester, Vermont, a New England mecca for skiers. He told me that living near a ski resort instantly increased the amount of entertaining and overnight guests he and his wife hosted. "Funny," he said, "we didn't seem to get this kind of foot traffic coming through our house when we lived in balmy Duluth, Minnesota!"

They've become adept at outdoor exploring, day trips in the Green Mountains, and big picnics on top of Mount Equinox.

Your area is probably full of untapped spots, both indoors and out, that could be great locations for your next party. Look in the Yellow Pages, read the local paper, and keep a running

HUNT UP A PARTY

"When my husband's extended family came to our neck of the woods for their annual reunion, we wanted to host some sort of party or event. However, with limited funds and space, throwing a gala or even renting a tent for our back yard (what back yard?) was out of the question. We put our thinking caps on, as desperate situations often call for, and came up with what we thought was a brilliant plan.

"We created a scavenger hunt in our area, which took a lot of legwork and creative thinking but not a lot of money or space. The family was divided into teams, children were eagerly included, and everyone split up with a goal in mind and their competitive natures piqued. After a few hours of gathering clues and souvenirs, we all met at a local Italian family restaurant, and each family picked up their own bill. The fun was in the hunt, not in keeping tabs of who paid for what, which was good because our little family was about all we could afford!"

Jennifer Gillis

list of possible ideas. Take advantage of the local tourist attractions near your home. They are always set up for crowds, serve food, and, in reality, you and your family probably don't enjoy them often anyway, since they are part of your everyday surroundings. If you live in New York City, for instance, take an outing to the Statue of Liberty with your guests. The boat ride is great fun by itself, and the history is fascinating. Entertaining can be educational, too!

Location, Location, Location

Reserve the pool at the YMCA or gym and swim for an hour with friends. Then have a pizza delivered there.

~

Have people meet at a park or nature reserve with their own picnics. This can be such a refreshing experience that you may want to make it a regular event, choosing different natural sites in your area.

~

Throw your party at a community Grange hall. The facility is usually quite spacious, and the price is right: sometimes a small rental fee, but often only a donation to the Grange or local 4-H club. The kitchen facilities are usually great as well.

If you can find an appropriate location, have a square dance. The music can be recorded, even the caller can be on tape, and since the focus is the dancing, the food needn't be abundant or fancy. In fact, if you can really get people into it, they will stay so busy they won't want to eat. And think of how good the exercise will be for everyone!

~

Rent a nearby bed-and-breakfast for your next family reunion. There are plenty of private bedrooms and baths, generally a large gathering room, and a fantastic breakfast every morning for the whole group. Best of all, no one has to do the linens, and you can stay in the comfort of your own home. We put 20 relatives into one "lodge" on Lake Champlain, and everyone was ecstatic about having his or her own space. We lived down the road, so it was an easy walk for them and for us, and we alternated homes for dinner. No one felt put out, and everyone pitched in.

~

If you really love to have parties, but just don't have the space for it, ask a good friend with a larger house if you can have the party there. Some people love the idea of having a party at their house without doing any of the work.

~

Picnics are always the greatest "simple" events. It's especially fun to go somewhere to picnic where you can gather some of the food, such as blueberries or apples. You might even gather fresh produce from your garden; tomatoes warmed by the sunshine and eaten whole are the best.

~

Have a hayride or sleigh ride. Rent the driver and wagon; you bring the food. Ask him or her to take you on local back roads, so that your ride can be leisurely and safe. Again, everyone can be responsible for something, so fun can be had by all.

~

Some summer camps rent their facilities after the season is over. This is usually very reasonably priced, and there is plenty of space for everyone. Plan a family reunion or group outing using the camp cabins. Rough it with campfire cookouts and easy breakfasts. Use the waterfront, hiking trails, and sporting facilities, making sure that someone is always on "safety patrol" where necessary. Sometimes the camp will provide lifeguards for an extra fee.

~

Meet at a soup kitchen or shelter with a group of friends and spend your time together helping others. You might be surprised just how much fun and how rewarding this kind of gathering can be.

~

White-water rafting, followed by a cookout, is a memorable way to entertain. With good gear and professional guides, this can be a great experience.

Go canoeing with your friends for a floating picnic. Make sure to scope out the river beforehand for safe places to "put in," spread your blankets, and enjoy your spread. I've done this on the Battenkill in Vermont, with just enough adventure and just enough relaxation. A "float" on tubes or rafts is a variation on this theme. My daughter's family does this in the Ozarks.

~

A cross-country ski outing can be wonderful fun with a group. If you are lucky enough to live where you can ski open trails, terrific. Take your picnic in thermos packs on your backs. If you ski on a groomed trail, there may be food facilities available for an extra fee.

~

The beach is always a special place to entertain, particularly as the day ends, the crowds clear, and the sun goes down. Remember, when you are at the beach, you need a big open blanket or portable table that allows you to spread out the food without worrying about getting sand on it. Try to pack things in lots of smaller packs, too: Lugging heavy coolers across the sand can be less than fun. Let everyone carry something smaller.

~

If the beach area allows, lobster and clam bakes are the perfect fare for beach parties. Dig your hole and build your fire, using plenty of seaweed once it is going. Wrap the lobsters, clams, corn on the cob, and potatoes in heavy-duty foil and let them steam in the open fire. When you are sure they are done, carefully remove them with heat-resistant gloves, pour melted butter into paper cups, and dig in! Make sure you remember the lobster-shell crackers or a hammer, or your meal can become very frustrating.

~

Entertaining on a boat can be wonderful fun, with the sun, wind, water, and quiet solitude that a lake can provide on a good day. Just remember to invite the right number of people for the boat you have, to have good safety gear like life jackets aboard, and to keep the alcohol consumption to a minimum. If your party goes on after dark, make sure there are plenty of lights on the boat.

~

Go with your group to play miniature golf. It is quite inexpensive, and people really get a kick out of the fun competitiveness of the game. If you mix up the teams (playing boys against girls, or switching dates), it really adds to the silliness. Any age can play, and after you are finished, go back home for the prize ceremony and a bite to eat.

~

Bowling is still a terrific sport for small or large groups. If your group is really large, with a little advance notice you can rent the bowling alley, closing it to outsiders. The staff can serve the food and drinks, and everyone can pay for shoes and games. Again, with something as much fun as bowling, the food takes a back seat to the event.

A group bike ride with a picnic packed on your backs is a great way to get some exercise, find some remote spot, and have some fun. If the food is too heavy to carry, have someone drive to the designated spot and drop off the goodies, spread the blankets, and prepare the feast for your arrival. Maybe that person can take the younger children with him or her as well. Just remember to save some energy for the ride home!

～

Several years ago my husband and I got together with five of our friends to plan a large "'50s Party." We met once a month to plan our joint guest list, and send out invitations to "come in the attire of the times and ready to party!" We rented a local hall, hired a disc jockey, bought plenty of soda, beer, chips, and pretzels, and waited for the day to arrive. When it finally did we had a ball. There were prizes for best costumes, best dancers, most authentic, cutest couple, and so on. We danced and sang throughout the night, served coffee and doughnuts, then headed for home and a good night's sleep. We had hired the janitor of the facility to clean up the next day so no one had to spend additional time. It was a wonderful event, inexpensive since we shared the cost six ways, and a great way to entertain a lot of people.

Remember, if you have your party somewhere other than your own home, the pressure of having to clean and cook for the crowd is off. All you need to do is plan, make a few phone calls, and have fun yourself.

11

Entertaining in Business

For the past 15 years, my husband and I have been partners in business. We own a small publishing company located in rural New England, and we publish books on things we like to do: gardening, cooking, herbal crafts, building, raising animals and kids. If we are not at work working, then we can generally be found at home working. For example, I am writing this book at home, which is going to be published by our company at work. Sometimes it's hard to distinguish our work life from our real life. Our work is our life, and we are fortunate because we both love it! While that may sound like it makes things easy, let me set you straight. We have actually had days when we've worked nearly 24 hours, and seven days a week is routine. Work is always on our minds and in our conversations.

Sometimes, with so many things going on in my life, I wonder if I can juggle everything successfully and still have some energy left for myself. Lots of us feel that way, I know, and finding a balance that works is key. If you get too busy, too tired, too tense, or have too many things to do, then nothing seems to get done well or completely, and the one who really suffers is you.

Luckily, my three grown children keep me from getting so self-absorbed that I'm too boring for others to be around. We travel a lot, our five grandchildren visit regularly, and each of the kids has a family dog that comes along. We have lots of friends who we love to see. We live in the small town where we went to college and the alumni crowd stops by often; thankfully, I love to entertain!

Since our business is so much a part of our life, we tend to entertain employees and clients often. Frequently we hold events at our home, ranging from a company picnic for 100 to a lunch for a particular work group or a dinner for a few out-of-town clients. We feel that bringing people into our home helps complete the picture for them, letting them know of our commitment to, and personal interest in, them. Through the years, I have learned a lot of tricks about business entertaining, and I am pleased to share them.

$\sim$

There are other small businesses in your area that are there to serve you. That is their business. Use their services often and wisely.

Keep a current supplier list at home or at work, and refer to it in the planning stages of your event. Organize the list by task — caterers, waitstaff, bartenders, housekeepers, liquor store, bakers, and so on — almost like the Yellow Pages. Just make sure you update it regularly. Keeping it on the computer makes it easy to add and delete things.

~

Call suppliers and ask them to send or fax you their menus, specialties, rates, special charges, and hours of operation. If they are good business people, they will automatically put you on their mailing lists and update you on their capabilities without your asking.

~

If you are entertaining in your home, interview the suppliers in person. Do it in your office for convenience, asking them to bring their important information with them. Ask them what they really love to do, what they are best at, what the best party was that they ever attended. Be sure to ask for references, and call them.

~

Have several suppliers that you can count on for the same thing, such as several caterers. Particularly during the busy seasons, your first choice may not be free to help you.

If you are planning a meal for a large group, either catered at home or at a restaurant, and you have never eaten the supplier's food, ask for a sample tasting in advance. The chef should be pleased to oblige and should offer to do it at no cost. When you are paying for a special event, you shouldn't have any surprises.

~

Recently, I planned a large dinner party for 60 employees. I used a local restaurant that could accommodate that crowd, but it had a new chef. I knew the menu I wanted to serve and how I thought it should be presented, so I spoke with the chef well in advance, giving him some of the recipes that I wanted to include. He was thrilled with my fresh approach and invited me and my husband, John, to sample the fare, along with different wines, several weeks before the actual event. He wanted to make sure everything would be just as I had imagined, so we went for dinner, on the house, and discussed everything in detail. I tweaked a few things and he made some more suggestions. He cared about my business, then and for the future. The party was a great success, and I never worried about a thing.

There is no greatness where there is not simplicity.

Leo Tolstoy

Be clear about how much you want to spend; for larger groups, ask for a discounted price on wine. You can determine its cost by asking your regular wine and liquor dealer, and taking markups into account. Buying 30 bottles of wine is much different from buying 1.

~

If you are doing business entertaining at home, you should usually be present before, during, and after dinner. Get the help you need to make this possible. If you have established a good working relationship with your help, and have put together a complete plan, then they should be able to manage fine without you in the kitchen.

~

If you are entertaining at a restaurant, the chef and waitstaff should also have a written plan from you so that there is no need for many detailed questions during the evening. We always invite the chef and staff to come out and say hello, to explain what they have done, and generally to receive a round of applause. This makes everyone feel great, and goes a long way toward assuring high quality the next time you use their services.

~

When entertaining a business client at home, ask your kids to say hello, then let them go off to their own rooms. Plan their meal and activities in advance so that they feel good about their evening.

If you are out to dinner with a client, try to sit in an area of the restaurant that is quiet enough for conversation. You don't want to have to shout to be heard, particularly if you are discussing sensitive business issues.

~

When the boss comes for dinner, be yourself. Whether you work for her or your spouse does, just remember that she is a normal human being and wants to enjoy her evening out. If you set a comfortable mood from the start, the evening will go well. Be as rested as you can be, and don't try to bite off more than you can comfortably chew.

~

Be prepared. Before the evening or lunch, do a little research on the people who will be with you. Where are they from? What is their role at their business? Is this a new or old client? Are there others in your own business who have dealt with this person or the company before? What was the relationship like? If you have done some homework, you won't feel like strangers, and the conversation can get off to a faster start.

~

If your spouse is bringing home a business client for dinner, or you are invited to go out with one, do some homework as well. The more prepared you are, the more relaxed you'll be.

When entertaining for business, keep all of your receipts so that you can document precisely your expenses (who? what? where? when? why?) and be reimbursed promptly. Make sure to ask your business office just how detailed you need to be on your reporting.

~

Entertaining for business needn't be boring or predictable. My husband and I once hosted a country cookout at our home with people from out of town, and they were thrilled to have been made to feel at home during an annual convention.

~

We have also entertained a large group of clients at a professional baseball game. We bought the tickets, and the Skydome did the rest! We've even had a birthday party at Wrigley Field, and it didn't even matter that our team didn't win.

~

We once took some other publishers and booksellers on an educational boat cruise down the Chicago River, too. Dinner was served while we learned about the history of this great city.

~

Business entertaining, personally and carefully done, can yield rich dividends and be a great "return on investment." It allows you to stand out from the pack.

Appendix

Entertaining Survey

We recently conducted a survey on entertaining at our company. About 40 people participated, ranging in age from 19 to 61. Both men and women responded, married and single, with and without children at home, all obviously working. This represents a good cross-section of today's society, and the interesting results follow:

1. **Do you like to entertain?**

Yes	63%
No	13%
Sometimes	25%

2. **How often do you entertain?**

Once a week	10%
Once a month	25%
Couple of times a month	38%
Couple of times a year	10%
Rarely	18%

3. **When you do entertain, which is your favorite day to entertain?**

Friday	15%
Saturday	63%
Sunday	18%
Weekday	5%

4. **Do you like to entertain large groups or small groups?**

Small	70%
Large	15%
Both	15%

5. **What is your favorite-size group to entertain?**

4	35%
6	15%
8	20%
12	30%
Bigger	10%

6. **Do you ask for help when you have guests over for dinner?**

Yes	38%
No	25%
Sometimes	38%

7. **Do you like to barbecue?**

Yes	80%
No	20%

8. **What is your favorite thing to barbecue?**

Chicken	30%
Steak	15%
Fish	10%
Seafood	10%
Veggies	20%
Pork	10%
Venison	5%

9. What is your favorite dessert to make?

Pie	15%
Cookies	10%
Cheesecake	23%
Brownics	13%
Ice cream	10%
Chocolate	25%

10. What is your favorite kind of dessert to eat?

Pie	13%
Cookies	0%
Cheesecake	10%
Ice cream	25%
Chocolate	40%
Cake	13%

11. What alcoholic drink do you serve most often?

Wine	45%
Beer	25%
Both	13%
Spirits	5%
All	5%
None	7%

12. Do you serve wine or beer with dinner?

Wine	45%
Beer	13%
Both	18%
None	12%
Nonalcoholic	12%

13. **What is your *least* favorite job related to entertaining at home?**

Shopping	15%
Planning	8%
Cleaning	30%
Dishes	23%
Cooking	15%
Other	9%

14. **What is your *favorite* job related to entertaining at home?**

Setting table	15%
Planning	20%
Decorating	15%
Cooking	25%
Introducing	13%
Conversation	5%

15. **What is your favorite main dish to cook for a dinner party?**

Chicken	35%
Pasta	28%
Seafood	13%
Roast	10%
Vegetarian	15%

16. **What is the main thing that keeps you from entertaining?**

Energy	20%
Time	38%
Money	18%
Space	10%
Cleaning	10%

17. **What is your favorite type of dish to bring to a potluck event?**

Bread	13%
Pasta	23%
Salad	15%
Beer/wine	15%
Appetizer	20%
We ask	5%

18. **Who do you prefer to entertain — family or friends? Or both equally?**

Family	13%
Friends	18%
Both	45%

19. **What's your favorite type of international cuisine?**

Italian	40%
Chinese	13%
French	8%
Japanese	10%
Thai	4%
Indian	4%
Mexican	13%

20. **Do you entertain more in any particular season?**

Winter	10%
Spring	5%
Summer	45%
Fall	8%
All year	18%
Holidays	15%

Index

Note: Page references in *italics* indicate illustrations; those in **boldface** indicate recipes.

Other Storey Titles
You Will Enjoy

Keeping Fitness Simple, by Porter Shimer. Provides reasons and ways to fit exercise into the reader's life, regardless of time, space, setting, or equipment. 160 pages. Paperback. ISBN 1-58017-034-X.

Keeping Life Simple, by Karen Levine. Offers hundreds of tips to take positive, effective control of your time, money, home, and life. 160 pages. Paperback. ISBN 0-88266-943-5.

Keeping Work Simple, by Don Aslett and Carol Cartaino. Provides tips for simplifying any work environment to achieve maximum job satisfaction and peak performance. 160 pages. Paperback. ISBN 0-88266-996-6.

The Stain and Spot Remover Handbook, by Jean Cooper. Explains how to treat stains caused by a variety of sources and how to avoid making a problem worse. 160 pages. Paperback. ISBN 0-88266-811-0.

Tea with Friends, by Elizabeth Knight. Presents a year's worth of occasions to bring friends together around a pot of tea. 64 pages. Hardcover. ISBN 1-58017-050-1.

Too Busy to Clean, by Patti Barrett. Offers hundreds of shortcuts and tricks for making cleaning more tolerable and less time consuming. 160 pages. Paperback. ISBN 1-58017-029-3.

These and other Storey books are available at your bookstore,
farm store, garden center, or directly from Storey Books,
Schoolhouse Road, Pownal, Vermont 05261,
or by calling 800-441-5700.
Visit our website at www.storey.com